Crochet Embellishments

by Jean Leinhauser

Leisure Arts, Inc.

Little Rock, Arkansas

Produced by

Production Team

Creative Directors: Jean Leinhauser and
    Rita Weiss
Technical Editor: Susan Lowman
Photographer: Carol Wilson Mansfield
Book Design: Joyce Lerner

Diagrams ©2007
by The Creative Partners™LLC
Reproduced by special permission

Published by Leisure Arts

© 2007 by Leisure Arts, Inc.,
5701 Ranch Drive
Little Rock, AR 72223
www. leisurearts.com

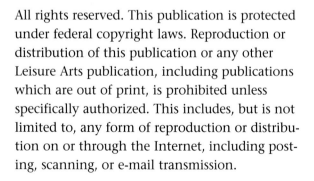

A Note from Jean

In this book you will find everything from glittering tassels to braids used in vintage Romanian lace to a heart motif you can sew on your sleeve.

Each chapter introduces another group of crocheted embellishments designed to add a special flair to your crocheted or knitted projects.

If you're looking for a crocheted bead to make a necklace, or a ruffled border for an afghan for your little princess, or a big red rose to accent your suit jacket, you will find it in these pages.

As you read through the patterns you'll notice a few things that are missing: most of the projects have no materials lists, and no hook or gauge specification. That's because you can work the patterns in any yarn you choose—from fine crochet cotton to bulky chenille—with any size hook that gives the effect you want.

Different yarns will give very different looks. The photo shows how one of our braids takes on a completely different personality when worked in size 3 crochet cotton, in sport weight yarn, and in worsted weight yarn. **Note:** *The instructions for making this braid are Braid 10 on page 58.*

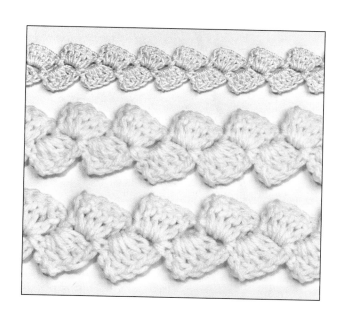

Except for the cords and braids, which we made in size 3 crochet cotton, the projects are all shown worked in sport or dk weight yarn. But you can have fun experimenting with different yarn textures and colors to create embellishments that are uniquely you.

And in case you can't remember how to crochet, or if you are confused about what those abbreviations and symbols mean, spend a little time with our Refresher Course staring on page 92. Then you'll be ready to start embellishing.

Jean Leinhauser
Creative Partners, LLC

Contents

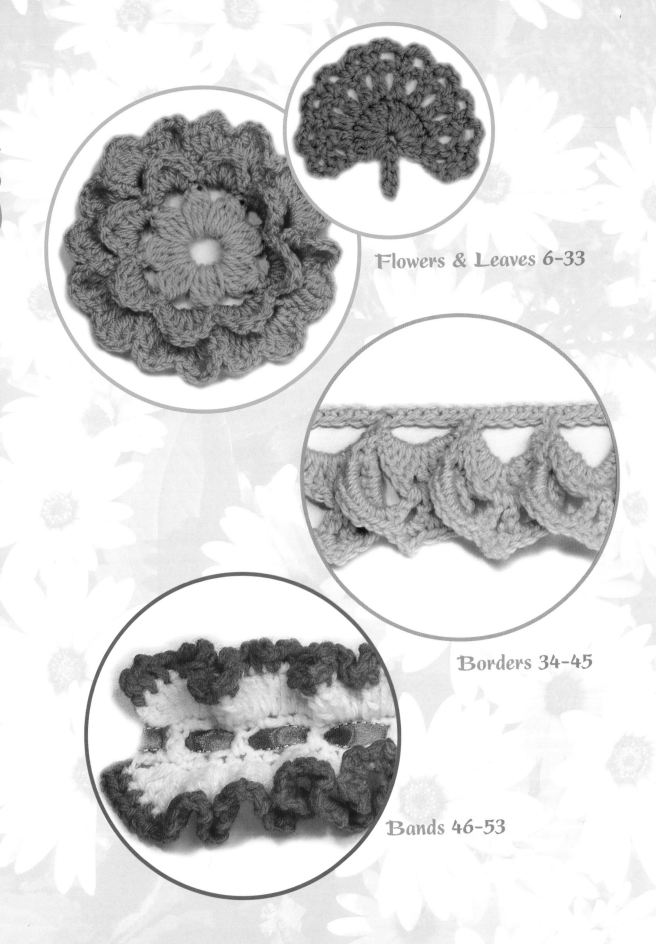

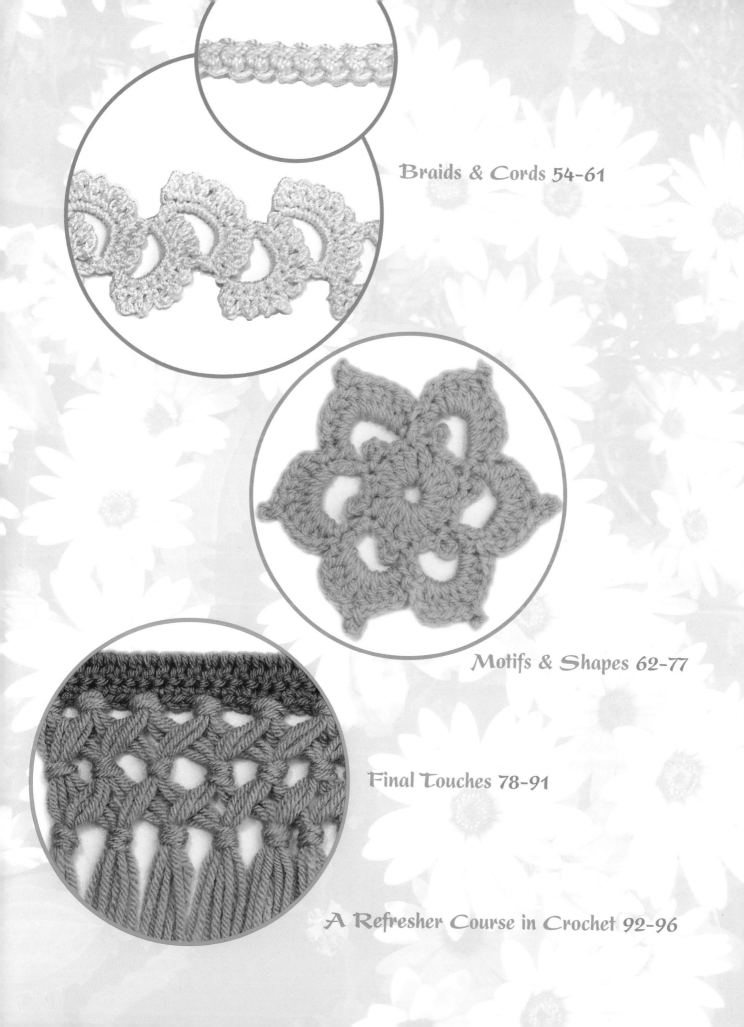

Flowers & Leaves

Flowers and leaves are fun to make, and are a great way to use up scrap yarn. The flowers are good for wearing as pins (craft stores carry pinbacks to which you can attach the flowers), or as decorations for packages or clothing. A small flower is a sweet addition to a child's dress or sweater. A group of flowers looks wonderful on a crocheted purse, or on a hat. A big flower on a curtain tieback adds drama. Our flowers are not botanically correct, so feel free to change their colors. Where there are flowers, there must be leaves, so we've given you a selection of various shapes and sizes.

Pink Bloom

Three colors:

Color A (yellow)

Color B (deep pink)

Color C (med pink)

Instructions

With Color A, ch 6, join with sl st to form a ring.

Rnd 1 (right side): Ch 5 (counts as a dc and ch-2 sp), dc in ring; (ch 2, dc in ring) 4 times, ch 2; join with sl st in 3rd ch of beg ch-5.

Rnd 2: Ch 1; *in next ch-2 sp work (sc, hdc, 3 dc, hdc, sc): petal made; rep from * around, join with sl st in beg sc. Finish off Color A.

Rnd 3: Turn piece to wrong side. Join Color B with sl st in back strands of center dc in any petal; * ch 4, sl st in back strands of center dc of next petal; rep from * around, ending last rep with ch 4, join in beg sl st; ch 1, turn piece to right side.

Rnd 4: *In next ch-4 sp work (sc, hdc, 2 dc, 1 tr, 2 dc, hdc, sc): petal made; rep from * around, join in beg sc. Finish off Color B.

Rnd 5: Turn piece to wrong side. Join Color C with sl st in back strands of tr of any petal ; * ch 5, sl st in back strands of center tr of next petal; rep from * around, ending last rep with ch 5, join in beg sl st; ch 1, turn piece to right side.

Rnd 6: *In next ch-5 sp work 8 sc; rep from * around, join with sc in beg sc.

Rnd 7: With right side facing, *ch 3 (equals a dc), dc in next sc, (ch 1, tr in next sc) 4 times, ch 1, dc in next sc, ch 3, sc in next sc; rep from * around; join in beg sc.

Finish off. Weave in yarn ends.

leave off last row

Dainty Daffy

Instructions

Ch 2.

Rnd 1: In 2nd ch from hook work 6 sc; join with sl st in back lp only of beg sc.

Rnd 2: Ch 3 (counts as first dc of rnd); working in back lp only of each st, (2 dc in next sc, dc in next sc) twice, 2 dc in last sc; join in top of beg ch-3: 9 dc. Finish off.

Rnd 3: Join yarn with sl st in any unused lp of Rnd 1; ch 1, 2 sc in same lp; work 2 sc in each rem lp around: 12 sc; join with sl st in beg sc.

Rnd 4: Ch 3; work (2 tr, ch 3, sl st) in same sc as joining, sl st in next sc; *in next sc work (sl st, ch 4, 2 tr, ch 4, sl st), sl st in next sc; rep from *around: 6 petals made; join. Finish off; weave in yarn ends.

Forget-Me-Not

Two colors:
Color A (yellow)
Color B (blue)

Instructions

With Color A, ch 5; join with sl st to form a ring.

Rnd 1: Ch 1, work 10 sc in ring; join with sl st in beg sc; finish off Color A.

Rnd 2: Join Color B with sl st in any sc; in same sc work (ch 3, 2 dc, ch 3, sl st), skip next sc; *in next sc work (sl st, ch 3, 2 dc, ch 3, sl st), skip next sc; rep from * 3 times more: 5 petals made; join with sl st in beg sl st. Finish off; weave in yarn ends.

Rosy Posies

Note: *The size of these rolled roses is determined by the length of the foundation chain. The chain for the smaller rose is given first, with the chain for the larger in parentheses.*

Instructions

Ch 15 (20).

Row 1: Work 2 dc in 2nd ch from hook; *3 dc in next ch; rep from * across; finish off, leaving a 6" yarn end.

Starting at beg of row, roll the row on itself, with the first sts made forming the center. Thread yarn end into a tapestry needle and stitch last dc to rest of rose.

Take several stitches completely through the rose to hold the roll in place.

9

Little Daisy

Two colors:

Color A (yellow)

Color B (white)

Stitch Guide

Cluster (CL): *YO twice; insert hook in specified st and draw up a lp; (YO and draw through 2 lps) twice; rep from * once more in same st; YO and draw through 3 lps: CL made.

Instructions

With Color A, ch 4, join with sl st to form a ring.

Rnd 1: Ch 1, work 8 sc in ring. Join in beg sc. Finish off Color A.

Rnd 2: Join Color B with sl st st in any sc; ch 4, work CL in same sc, ch 4, sl st in same sc; *sl st in next sc, ch 4, CL in same sc, ch 4, sl st in same sc; rep from * around: 8 petals made; join with sl st in beg sl. Finish off; weave in yarn ends.

Cockscomb

Two colors:

Color A (yellow)

Color B (pink)

Instructions

With Color A, ch 4, join with sl st to form a ring.

Rnd 1: Ch 1, work 6 sc in ring; do not join.

Rnd 2: Work 2 sc in each sc: 12 sc; join with sl st in beg sc; finish off Color A.

Rnd 3: Join Color B with sl st in any sc; ch 1, work 3 sc in same sc as joining and in each rem sc: 36 sc; join with sl st in beg sc.

Rnd 4: Ch 3, dc in joining; work 2 dc in each rem sc: 72 dc; join with sc in top of beg ch-3.

Rnd 4: *Ch 3, sc in next dc; rep from * around ending with ch 3; join in top of beg ch-3. Finish off; weave in yarn ends.

Cornflower

Two colors:

Color A (yellow)

Color B (med blue).

Instructions

With Color A, ch 6, join with sl st to form a ring.

Rnd 1: Ch 1; in ring work (sc, ch 2) 8 times; join in beg sc; finish off Color A.

Rnd 2: Join Color B in any ch-2 sp; ch 3 (counts as a dc), 3 dc in same sp; ch 3, turn; dc in first dc (at base of turning ch), dc in next 2 dc and in top of beg ch-3: 5-dc petal made; ch 3, turn; *working behind petal just made, work 4 dc in next ch-2 sp, ch 3, turn; dc in first dc (at base of turning ch), dc in next 3 dc: 5 –dc petal made; ch 3, turn; rep from * around, ending last rep with join with sl st in top of beg ch-3.

Finish off; weave in yarn ends.

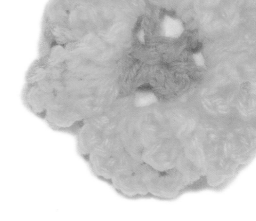

Ruffled Blossom

Two colors:

Color A (orange)

Color B (gold)

Instructions

With Color A, ch 6, join with sl st to form a ring.

Rnd 1: Ch 5 (counts as a dc and ch-2 sp), dc in ring; *ch 2, dc in ring; rep from * 4 times more, ch 2, join with sl st in 3rd ch of beg ch-5: 6 ch-2 sps. Finish off Color A.

Rnd 2: Join Color B with sl st in any ch-2 sp; ch 1, in same sp work (sc, hdc, 3 dc, hdc, sc); * in next ch-2 sp work (sc,hdc, 3 dc, hdc, sc); rep from * around, join with sl st in beg sc.

Rnd 3: *Ch 3, sl st in next st; rep from * around; join in beg sl st. Finish off; weave in yarn ends.

Blooming Beauty

Three colors:
Color A (yellow)
Color B (gold)
Color C (bright pink)

Instructions

With Color A, ch 5, join with sl st to form a ring.

Rnd 1: Sl st in ring; ch 5 (counts as a tr and ch-1 sp), tr in ring; (ch 1, tr in ring) 10 times, ch 1, join in 4th ch of beg ch-5.

Rnd 2: Ch 1, sc in joining; *2 sc in next ch-1 sp, sc in next tr; rep from * around, ending last rep with 2 sc in last ch-1 sp; join in beg sc. Finish off Color A.

Rnd 3: Join Color B with sc in front lp only of any sc; *ch 3, sc in front lp only of next sc; rep from * around, ending last rep with ch 3, join in beg sc. Finish off Color B.

Rnd 4: Working behind Rnd 3 and in unused lps of Rnd 2, join Color C with sc in any lp; *ch 3, skip 2 lps, sc in next lp; rep from * around, ending last rep with ch 3, sl st in beg sc: 12 ch-3 lps.

Rnd 5: *In next ch-3 lp work shell of (hdc, 2 dc, 2 tr, 2 dc, hdc), sl st in next sc; rep from * around, ending last rep with sl st in beg sc. Finish off; weave in yarn ends.

Puffy Petals

Two colors:
Color A (dk pink)
Color B (yellow)

Stitch Guide

Popcorn Stitch (Pst): Work 4 dc in specified sp; drop lp from hook, insert hook from front to back in top of first dc made, pick up dropped lp and draw through: Pst made.

Instructions

With Color A, ch 6, join with sl st to form a ring.

Rnd 1: Ch 1, work 12 sc in ring; join with sc in first sc.

Rnd 2: *Ch 2, skip next sc, sc in next sc; rep from * around, ending last rep with ch 2, join in beg sc: 6 ch-2 sps. Finish off Color A.

Rnd 3: Join Color B with sl st in any ch-2 sp; in same sp work (ch 3, Pst, ch 3, sl st); *in next ch-2 sp work (sl st, ch 3, Pst, ch 3, sl st); rep from * around, join. Finish off Color B; weave in yarn ends.

Fancy Flora

Instructions

Ch 4, join with sl st to form a ring.

Rnd 1: Ch 3 (counts as a dc), work 9 dc in ring: 10 dc; join with sc in 3rd ch of beg ch-3.

Rnd 2: Sc in each dc around: 10 sc; join in beg sc. **Note:** Work will tend to turn to wrong side; push so right side is facing you.

Rnd 3: *Ch 2, skip next sc, sc in next sc; rep from * around, ending last rep with ch 2, join in beg sc: 5 ch-2 spaces.

Rnd 4: In each ch-2 sp work petal of (sl st, ch 2, 4 dc, ch 2, sl st); join in beg sl st: 5 petals made.

Rnd 5: Ch 1; working behind petals of Rnd 4, *sc in back lp of next skipped sc on Rnd 3, ch 4; rep from * around, join in beg sc: 5 ch-4 lps.

Rnd 6: In each ch-4 lp work petal of (sl st, ch 2, 7 dc, ch 2, sl st): 5 petals made; join in beg sl st.

Rnd 7: Ch 2; working behind petals of Rnd 6, *sl st in back strands of center dc of next petal on Rnd 6, ch 5; rep from * around, join in beg sl st.

Rnd 8: In each ch-5 lp work petal of (sl st, ch 2, 9 dc, ch 2, sl st); join in beg sl st: 5 petals made. Finish off; weave in yarn ends.

Petite Flora

Instructions

Ch 4, join with sl st to form a ring.

Rnd 1: Ch 1, work 12 sc in ring; join with sl st in beg sc.

Rnd 2: *Ch 4, sl st in next sc; rep from * around, end last rep with sl st in beg sl st. Finish off; weave in yarn ends.

Sunny Flower

Two colors:

Color A (orange)

Color B (gold)

Instructions

With Color A, ch 4.

Rnd 1: Work 11 dc in 4th ch from hook; join with sl st in top of beg ch.

Rnd 2: Ch 3 (counts as first dc of rnd), dc in joining; work 2 dc in each st around; join with sl st in top of beg ch: 24 dc. Finish off Color A.

Rnd 3: Join Color B with sc in any dc; *ch 20, sc in next dc; rep from * around, ending last rep with sl st in beg sc. Finish off; weave in yarn ends.

Dandelion

Instructions

Ch 10; join with sl st to form a ring.

Rnd 1: Ch 1, work 12 sc in ring; join in front lp only of beg sc.

Rnd 2 (right side): Working entire rnd in front lp only of each st, in beg sc work (ch 6, sc in same sc) twice ; *sc in next sc, (ch 6, sc in same sc) twice ; rep from * around, join in beg sc.

Rnd 3: Turn piece to wrong side. Working in unused back lps of Rnd 2, *sc in next lp, (ch 6, sc in same lp) twice; rep from around; join in beg sc. Finish off. Weave in yarn ends.

Purple Aster

Two colors:

Color A (yellow)

Color B (purple)

Instructions

With Color A, ch 6, join with sl st to form a ring.

Rnd 1: Ch 1, work 12 sc in ring; join with sl st in front lp only of beg sc.

Rnd 2: Working in front lps only, ch 3, sl st in same sc as joining; *sl st in front lp only of next sc, ch 3, sl st in front lp only of same sc; rep from * around, join in beg sc. Finish off Color A.

Rnd 3: Join Color B with sl st in unused back lp of any sc of Rnd 2, ch 8, sl st in same lp; *sl st in back lp of next sc, ch 12, sl st in same lp; **sl st in back lp of next sc, ch 8, sl st in same lp; rep from * around, ending last rep at **; join, finish off Color B. Weave in yarn ends.

Daisies

Two colors:

Color A (lime green)

Color B (yellow or lavender)

Instructions

With Color A, ch 8 join with sl st to form a ring.

Rnd 1: Ch 1, work 12 sc in ring; join. Finish off Color A.

Rnd 2: Join Color B with sl st in any sc; in same sc work (ch 3, 3 dc, ch 3, sl st) ; *skip next sc, in next sc work (sl st, ch 3, 3 dc, ch 3, sl st); rep from * around, ending last rep with skip last sc, join in beg sl st. Finish off; weave in yarn ends.

Looped Petals

Two colors:

Color A (yellow)

Color B (lavender)

Instructions

With Color A, ch 6, join with sl st to form a ring.

Rnd 1: Ch 1, work 13 sc in ring; join in beg sc. Finish off Color A.

Rnd 2: Join Color B with sl st in any sc, ch 12, sl st in same sc; *sl st in next sc, ch 12, sl st in same sc; rep from * around, join in beg sc. Finish off; weave in yarn ends.

Wavy Petals

Two colors:

Color A (gold)

Color B (deep pink)

Instructions

With Color A, ch 5, join with sl st to form a ring.

Rnd 1: Sl st in ring; ch 6 (counts as a tr and ch-2 sp), tr in ring; (ch 2, tr in ring) 10 times, ch 2, join with sc in 4th ch of beg ch-6: 12 tr and 12 ch-2 sps.

Rnd 2: * Work 2 sc in next ch-2 sp, sc in next tr; rep from * around, ending last rep with 2 sc in last ch-2 sp: 36 sc; join with sc in beg sc.

Rnd 3: *Ch 3, skip next sc, sc in next sc; rep from * around, ending last rep with join with sl st in beg sc: 18 ch-3 sps. Finish off Color A.

Rnd 4: Join Color B in any ch-3 sp; ch 3 (counts as a dc), work 7 dc in same sp; *work 8 dc in next ch-3 sp; rep from * around, join with sc in 3rd ch of beg ch-3.

Rnd 5: *Ch 2, skip next dc, sc in next dc; rep from * around, ending last rep with sl st in joining sc. Finish off; weave in yarn ends.

Royal Rose

Instructions

Ch 5, join with sl st to form a ring.

Rnd 1 (right side): *In ring work (sc, 3 dc, sc): petal made; rep from *3 times more: 4 petals made; join with sl st in beg sc.

Rnd 2: Ch 1; *working behind petals of Rnd 1, sc in back strands of first sc of next petal, ch 4, sc in back strands of last sc of same petal; rep from * 3 times more, join with sl st in beg sc: four ch-4 lps.

Rnd 3: *In next ch-4 lp work (sc, dc, tr, dc, sc, dc, tr, dc, sc): 2 petals made; rep from * 3 times more: 8 petals made; do not join.

Rnd 4: Working behind petals of Rnd 3, sc in back strands of first sc of next petal; *ch 4, sc in back strands of next sc; rep from * around, ending last rep with ch 4, join in beg sc: 8 ch-4 lps.

Rnd 5: *In next ch-4 lp work (sl st, ch 3, 4 dc, ch 3, sl st): petal made; rep from * around, join with sl st in beg sl st: 8 petals made. Finish off; weave in yarn ends.

Cone Flower

Two colors:

Color A (rose)

Color B (yellow)

Instructions

Rnd 1: With Color A, ch 2, work 8 sc in 2nd ch from hook; do not join, mark beg of rnds.

Rnd 2: Work 2 sc in each sc around: 16 sc; do not join.

Rnd 3: Sc in each sc around, do not join.

Rnd 4: Rep Rnd 3 but at end of rnd join with sl st in beg sc. Finish off Color A.

Rnd 5: Join Color B with sc in any sc; *ch 2, skip next sc, sc in next sc; rep from *around, ending last rep with ch 2, join with sl st in beg sc: 8 ch-2 sps.

Rnd 6: *In next ch-2 sp work petal of (sc, hdc, dc, 2 tr, dc, hdc, sc); rep from *around, join in beg sc. Finish off; weave in yarn ends.

Pinkie

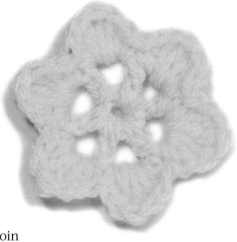

Two colors:

Color A (yellow)

Color B (pink)

Instructions

With Color A, ch 6; join to form a ring.

Rnd 1: Work 12 sc in ring; join with sl st in beg sc.

Rnd 2: Ch 5 (counts as a dc and ch-2 sp), (dc in ring, ch 2) 5 times; join with sl st in 3rd ch of beg ch-3: 6 ch-2 sps. Finish off Color A.

Rnd 3: Join Color B with sl st in any ch-2 sp; in same sp work (sc, hdc, 3 dc, hdc, sc): petal made; work petal in each rem ch-2 sp; join with sl st in beg sc. Finish off; weave in yarn ends.

A Little Lavender

Two Colors:

Color A (off white)

Color B (lavender)

Instructions

With Color A, ch 6, join with sl st to form a ring.

Rnd 1 (right side): * In ring work (sc, 4 dc, sc): petal made; rep from * twice more, join with sl st in beg sc: 3 petals made.

Rnd 2: Ch 2; working behind petals, *sc in back strands of center 2 dc sts of next petal; ch 3, sc in back strands of next sc; ch 3; rep from * around: 6 ch-3 sps; join with sc in beg sc.

Rnd 3: *In next ch-3 sp work petal of (sl st, ch 3, 5 dc, ch 3, sl st), sc in next sc; rep from * around; join in beg sl st.

Rnd 4: Working behind petals of Rnd 3, sc around next sc of Rnd 2; ch 6, *sc around next sc, ch 6; rep from * around: 6 ch 6 sps; join.

Rnd 5: *In next ch-6 sp work (sl st , ch 3, 7 dc, ch 3, sl st) sc in next sc; rep from * around; join. Finish off; weave in yarn ends.

Borders

Rnd 5 Border: With right side facing, join Color B with sc in any sc of Rnd 5; * ch 3, sc in top of each of next 7 dc, ch 3, sc in next sc; rep from * around, ending last rep with join, finish off.

Rnd 3 Border: With right side facing, join Color B with sc in any sc of Rnd 3; *ch 3, sc each of next 5 dc, ch 3, sc in next sc; in sl rep from * around, join. Finish off; weave in yarn ends.

Bold Bloom

Two Colors:

Color A (lime green)

Color B (bright pink)

Stitch Guide

Cluster (CL): *YO, insert hook in ring and draw up a lp to height of a dc, YO and draw through 2 lps; rep from * 3 times more, YO and draw through 4 lps: CL made.

Instructions

With Color A, ch 8, join with sl st to form a ring.

Rnd 1 (right side): Ch 3; *work CL in ring, ch 3; rep from * 7 times more, join with sl st in top of first CL: 8 ch-3 sps; finish off Color A.

Rnd 2: Join Color B with sc in any ch-3 sp between CLs; in same sp work (hdc, 2 dc, tr, 2 dc, hdc, sc): petal made; * in next ch-3 sp between CLs work petal of (sc,hdc, 2 dc, tr, 2 dc, hdc, sc); rep from * around, join in beg sc: 8 petals made.

Rnd 3: Ch 2; turn piece to wrong side; *sc in back strands of next sc to right, ch 3, sc in back strands of next tr, ch 3; rep from * around, join: 16 ch-3 sps.

Rnd 4: Turn piece to right side; in each ch-3 sp work petal of (sc, hdc, dc, tr, dc, hdc, sc): 16 petals made; join. Finish off, weave in yarn ends.

Irish Crochet Rose

Stitch Guide

Front Post Single Crochet (FPsc): Insert hook from front to back to front around post (vertical bar) of specified st and draw up a lp, YO and draw through both lps on hook: FPsc made.

Instructions

Ch 8, join with sl st to form a ring.

Rnd 1: Ch 1, work 16 sc in ring; join in beg sc.

Rnd 2: Ch 6 (counts as a dc and ch-3 sp), skip next sc, dc in next sc; (ch 3, skip next sc, dc in next sc) 6 times; ch 3, skip next sc, join in 3rd ch of beg ch-6: eight ch-3 lps.

Rnd 3: *In next ch-3 sp work (sc,hdc, 3 dc, hdc, sc): petal made; rep from * around: 8 petals made; join in beg sc. Finish off.

Rnd 4: Working behind petals of Rnd 3, join yarn with FPsc around any dc of Rnd 2; *ch 4, FPsc around next dc; rep from * around, ending last rep with ch 4, join in beg sc: 8 ch-4 lps.

Rnd 5: *In next ch-4 lp work petal of (sc, hdc, 4 dc, hdc, sc); rep from * around, join with sl st in beg sc. Finish off.

Marigold

Two colors:

Color A (gold)

Color B (orange)

Stitch Guide

Cluster (CL): *YO, insert hook in specified lp and draw up a lp to height of a dc; YO and draw through 2 lps on hook; rep from * 2 times more in same lp, YO and draw through 4 lps: CL made.

Instructions

Rnd 1: With Color A, ch 4; work 11 dc in 4th ch from hook; join with sl st in top of beg ch: 12 dc.

Rnd 2: Ch 3 (counts as a dc), dc in base of ch; work 2 dc in each dc around; join with sc in top of beg ch: 24 dc.

Rnd 3: *Ch 3, skip 3 dc, sc in next dc; rep from * around, ending last rep with ch 3, join with sl st in beg sc: 6 ch-3 sps. Finish off Color A.

Rnd 4: Join Color B with sc in any ch-3 lp; ch 3, CL in same lp; (ch 3, CL in same lp) two times more; ch 3; * in next ch-3 lp work (CL,ch 3) 3 times; rep from * around, join with sl st in top of beg CL. Finish off Color B; weave in yarn ends.

Sign of Spring

Two colors:

Color A (yellow)

Color B (lavender)

Instructions

With Color A, ch 6, join with sl st to form a ring.

Rnd 1: Ch 1, work 12 sc in ring; join with sl st in beg sc.

Rnd 2: Ch 3 (counts as a dc), dc in base of ch; work 2 dc in each sc around: 24 dc; join with sc in top of beg ch-3.

Rnd 3: *Ch 3, skip next dc, sc in next dc; rep from * around, ending last rep with ch 3, join in beg sc. Finish off Color A.

Rnd 4: Join Color B with sl st in any ch-3 sp; ch 3, (counts as a dc), in same sp work(3 dc, 2 tr, 4 dc); * in next ch-3 sp work (4 dc, 2 tr, 4 dc); rep from * around, join with sl st in top of beg ch-3. Finish off; weave in yarn ends.

Fanciful Flower

Four colors:

Color A (lime green)

Color B (yellow)

Color C (purple)

Color D (lavender).

Instructions

Rnd 1: With Color A, ch 5 (counts as a dc and ch-1 sp); in 5th ch from hook work (dc, ch 1) 5 times; join in 4th ch of beg ch-5: six ch-1 sps. Finish off Color A.

Rnd 2: Join Color B with sc in any ch-1 sp, in same sp work (hdc, 2 dc, hdc, sc): petal made; *in next ch-1 sp work petal of (sc, hdc, 2 dc, hdc, sc); rep from * around, join with sl st in beg sc. Finish off Color B.

Rnd 3: Working behind petals of Rnd 2, join Color C with sl st in strands at back of center 2 dc sts of any petal; *ch 4, join with sl st in strands at back of center 2 dc sts of next petal; rep from * around, ending last rep with ch 4, join with sl st in beg sl st; 6 ch-4 sps.

Rnd 4: *In next ch-4 sp work petal of (sc, hdc, 4 dc, hdc, sc); rep from * around, join with sl st in beg sc. Finish off Color C.

Rnd 5: Working behind petals of Rnd 4, join Color D with sl st in strands at back of center 2 dc of any petal; *ch 5, sl st in strands at back of center 2 dc of next petal; rep from * around, ending last rep with sl st in beg sl st.

Rnd 6: *In next ch-5 sp work petal of (sc, hdc, 2 dc, 2 tr, 2 dc, hdc, sc); rep from * around, join with sl st in beg sc. Finish off Color D; weave in yarn ends.

Pansy

Three colors:

Color A (yellow)

Color B (purple)

Color C (lavender)

Instructions

Rnd 1: With Color A, ch 2, work 5 sc in 2nd ch from hook. Finish off Color A.

Rnd 2: Join Color B with sl st in any sc; (ch 8, sl st in next sc) twice; ch 6, sl st in next sc, ch 7, sl st in next sc, ch 6, join with sc in beg ch-8 lp.

Top Petals: In same ch-8 lp work [hdc, dc, tr, (ch 1, tr) 9 times, dc, hdc, sc]; in next ch-8 lp work [sc, hdc, dc, tr, (ch 1, tr) 9 times, dc, hdc sc]. Finish off Color B.

Bottom Petals: Join Color C with sc in next ch-6 lp; in same lp work (hdc, 6 dc, hdc, sc); in next ch-7 lp work (sc, hdc, 7 dc, hdc, sc); in next ch-6 lp work (sc, hdc, 6 dc, hdc, sc).

Finish off Color C; weave in yarn ends.

Tipped Petals

Two colors:

Color A (yellow)

Color B (pink)

Stitch Guide

Popcorn (PC): Work 4 dc in ring; drop lp from hook, insert hook from front to back in top of first dc worked, insert hook in dropped lp and draw through, ch 1: PC made.

Instructions

With Color A, ch 8; join with sl st to form a ring.

Rnd 1: Sl st in ring, ch 3; (work PC in ring, ch 2) 8 times; join in top of beg PC.

Finish off Color A.

Rnd 2: Join Color B in any ch-2 sp; *ch 8, sl st in 2nd ch from hook, sc in next ch, hdc in next ch, dc in each of next 3 chs, hdc in last ch, sl st in next ch-2 sp; rep from * around, ending last rep with join in beg sl st. Finish off; weave in yarn ends.

Blue Beauty

3 colors:

Color A (yellow)

Color B (med blue)

Color C (lt blue)

Instructions

With Color A, ch 6, join with sl st to form a ring.

Rnd 1: Ch 1, work 12 sc in ring; join in beg sc. Finish off Color A.

Rnd 2: Working in front lps only, join Color B with sl st in front lp of any sc; ch 12, sl st in same sc; *sl st in front lp of next sc, ch 12, sl st in same sc; rep from * around, join in beg sl st. Finish off Color B.

Rnd 3: Working in back lps only, join Color C with sl st in back lp of any sc on Rnd 1; *ch 20, sl st in same sc, sl st in next sc; rep from * around, join in beg sl st. Finish off Color C; weave in yarn ends.

Sweet Summer

Two Colors:

Color A (gold)

Color B (pink)

Instructions

With Color A, ch 6, join with sl st to form a ring.

Rnd 1: Sl st in ring; ch 3 (counts as a dc), work 15 dc in ring: 16 dc. Finish off Color A.

Rnd 2: Join Color B with sc in any dc; *work 5 dc in next dc, sc in next dc; rep from * around, ending last rep with 5 dc in last dc; join with sc in beg sc.

Rnd 3: *(Sc in next dc, ch 1) 4 times, sc in next dc, sc in next sc; rep from * around, ending last rep with join with sl st in beg sc. Finish off Color B; weave in yarn ends.

Bluette

3 colors:

Color A (gold)

Color B (med blue)

Color C (lt blue).

Instructions

With Color A, ch 4, join with sl st to form a ring.

Rnd 1: Sl st in ring; ch 4 (equals a dc and ch-1 sp), (dc in ring, ch 1) 7 times, join in 3rd ch of beg ch-4: 8 ch-1 sps. Finish off Color A.

Rnd 2: Join Color B in any ch-1 sp; ch 3, dc in same sp; *ch 2, 2 dc in next ch-1 sp; rep from * around, ending last rep with ch 2, join in top of beg ch-3.

Rnd 3: Sl st in next dc and into next ch-2 sp; in same sp work (sc, ch 6, sc), ch 3; * in next ch 2 sp work (sc, ch 6, sc), ch 3; rep from * around, join in beg sc. Finish off Color B.

Rnd 4: Join Color C with sc in any ch 3 sp; *work 12 dc in next ch-6 sp, sc in next ch-3 sp; rep from * around, ending last rep with join in beg sc. Finish off Color C; weave in yarn ends.

Leaves

Leaf 1

Instructions

Ch 10.

Rnd 1: Sc in 2nd ch from hook, hdc in each of next 2 chs, dc in each of next 5 chs, 10 tr in last ch; working now in unused lps on opposite side of ch, dc in each of next 5 lps, hdc in each of next 2 lps, sc in last lp, join with sl st in beg sc. Ch 4 for stem, sl st in 2nd ch from hook and in next 2 chs; join with sl st in first st of rnd. Finish off; weave in yarn ends.

Leaf 2

Instructions

Ch 8.

Rnd 1: Sc in 2nd ch from hook, hdc in next ch, dc in each of next 4 chs, work 10 tr in next ch; working now in unused lps on opposite side of ch, dc in each of next 4 lps, hdc in next 2 lps, join with sl st in beg sc. Ch 4 for stem, sl st in 2nd ch from hook and in next 2 chs; join with sl st in first st of rnd. Finish off; weave in yarn ends.

Leaf 3

Instructions

Ch 18.

Rnd 1: Sl st in 2nd ch from hook, sc in next 2 chs, hdc in next 2 chs, dc in next 2 chs, 2 dc in next ch; tr in next 2 chs; dc in next 2 chs, hdc in next 2 chs, sc in next 2 chs, in next ch work (sc, ch 1, sc); working now on opposite side of ch in unused lps, sc in next 2 chs, hdc in next 2 chs, dc in 2 chs, tr in 2 chs, 2 dc in next ch; dc in 2 chs, hdc in 2 chs, sc in 2 chs; sl st in next ch; join with sl st in beg sl st.

Rnd 2: Sl st first st, sc in each st along first side of ch to ch-2 sp, work 3 sc in ch-2 sp; sc in each st along opposite side of ch to last st, sl st in last st, join. Finish off; weave in yarn ends.

Leaf 4

Instructions

Ch 10.

Row 1: Sl st in 2nd ch from hook and in next ch; sc in next 2 chs, dc in next 2 chs, 3 dc in next ch; hdc in next ch, sc in last ch. Finish off; weave in yarn ends.

Leaf 5

Instructions

Ch 8, join with sl st to form a ring.

Rnd 1: In ring work (sc, 2 hdc, 6 dc, 2 tr, 6 dc, 2 hdc, sc); ch 7 for stem, sl st in 2nd ch from hook and in next 5 chs, join with sl st in beg sc. Finish off; weave in yarn ends.

Leaf 6

Instructions

Ch 6, join with sl st to form a ring.

Rnd 1: In ring work sc, 2 hdc, 5 dc, tr, 5 dc, 2 hdc, sc; ch 5 for stem,sl st in 2nd ch from hook and in next 3 chs, join with sl st in beg sc. Finish off; weave in yarn ends.

Leaf 7

Instructions

Ch 4.

Rnd 1: Work 11 dc in 4th ch from hook; join with sl st in top of beg ch-4.

Rnd 2: Ch 3, dc in joining; 2 dc in each dc around: 24 dc; join in 3rd ch of beg ch-3; ch 5 for stem, sl st in 2nd ch from hook and in next 3 chs; join.

Finish off, weave in yarn ends.

Leaf 8

Instructions

Ch 4.

Rnd 1: Work 15 dc in 4th ch from hook; join with sl st in top of beg ch-4.

Rnd 2: Ch 3, dc in joining; 2 dc in each dc around: 32 dc; join in 3rd ch of beg ch-3; ch 8 for stem, sl st in 2nd ch from hook and in next 6 chs; join.

Finish off; weave in yarn ends.

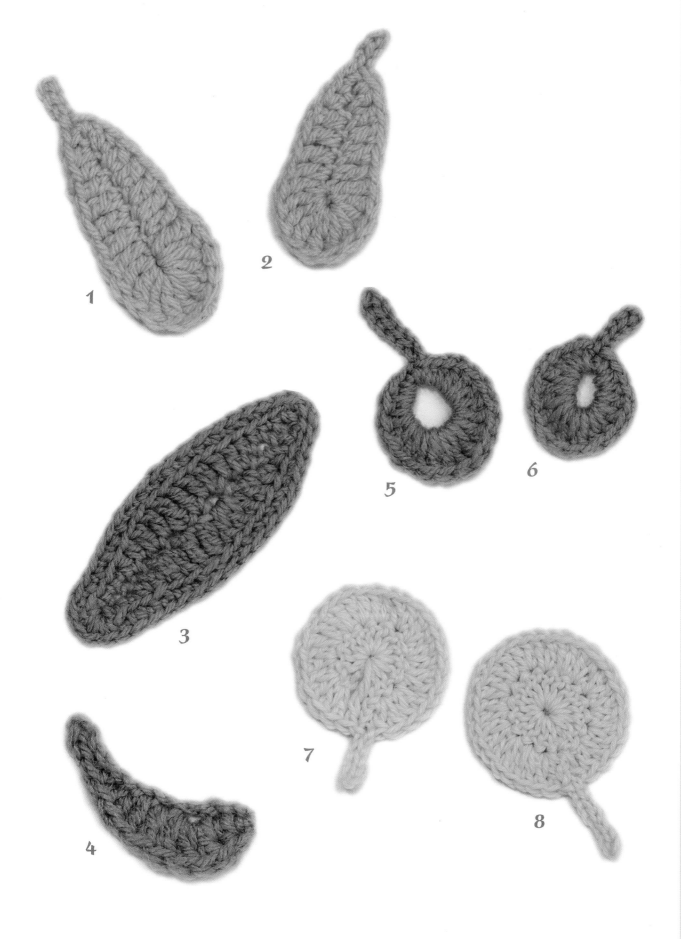

1

2

3

4

5

6

7

8

Leaf 9

Instructions

Ch 4, join with sl st to form a ring.

Row 1: Sl st into ring, ch 3, work 5 dc in ring; do not join; ch 3, turn.

Row 2: Dc in base of ch; 2 dc in each rem dc; ch 1, turn.

Row 3: Sc in first dc, *ch 2; sc in next dc; rep from * across, ending with ch 2, sc in 3rd ch of turning ch. Finish off; weave in yarn ends.

Leaf 10

Instructions

Ch 6, join with sl st to form a ring.

Row 1: Sl st into ring, ch 3, work 8 dc in ring; do not join; ch 3, turn.

Row 2: Dc in base of ch; 2 dc in each rem dc; ch 1, turn.

Row 3: Sc in first dc; *ch 2, sc in next dc; rep from * across, ending with ch 2, sc in 3rd ch of turning ch. Finish off; weave in yarn ends.

Leaf 11

Instructions

Ch 5.

Row 1: Sl st in 2nd ch from hook and in next 3 chs; ch 3 (counts as a dc on following row).

Row 2: Work 11 dc in base of ch; ch 4 (counts as a dc and ch-1 sp on following row), turn.

Row 3: *Dc in next dc, ch 1; rep from * across, ending last rep with dc in last dc; ch 1, turn.

Row 4: Sc in first dc; *ch 2, sc in next dc; rep from * across. Finish off; weave in yarn ends.

Leaf 12

Instructions

Ch 11.

Rnd 1: Sc in 2nd ch from hook and in next ch; hdc in next ch, dc in each of next 4 chs, hdc in next ch, sc in next ch, work 3 sc in last ch; working now in unused lps on opposite side of foundation ch, sc in next lp, hdc, in next lp, dc in each of next 4 lps, hdc in next lp, sc in each of last 2 lps; join in beg sc.

Rnd 2: *Ch 1, sc in next st; rep from * around, join. Finish off; weave in yarn ends.

Leaf 13

Instructions

Ch 2.

Row 1: Work 3 sc in 2nd ch from hook; ch 1, turn.

Row 2: Work 2 sc in first sc, sc in next sc, 2 sc in last sc: 5 sc; ch 1, turn.

Row 3: Work 2 sc in first sc, sc in next 3 sc, 2 sc in last sc: 7 sc; ch 1, turn.

Rows 4 through 9: Sc in each sc; ch 1, turn.

Row 10: Draw up a lp in each of first 2 sc, YO and draw through 3 lps: dec made; Sc in each sc to last 2 sc, draw up a lp in each of next 2 sc, YO and draw through 3 lps: dec made: 5 sc; ch 1, turn.

Row 11: Rep Row 10: 3 sc; ch 1, turn.

Row 12: Draw up a lp in each rem sc, YO and draw through 4 lps. Finish off; weave in yarn ends.

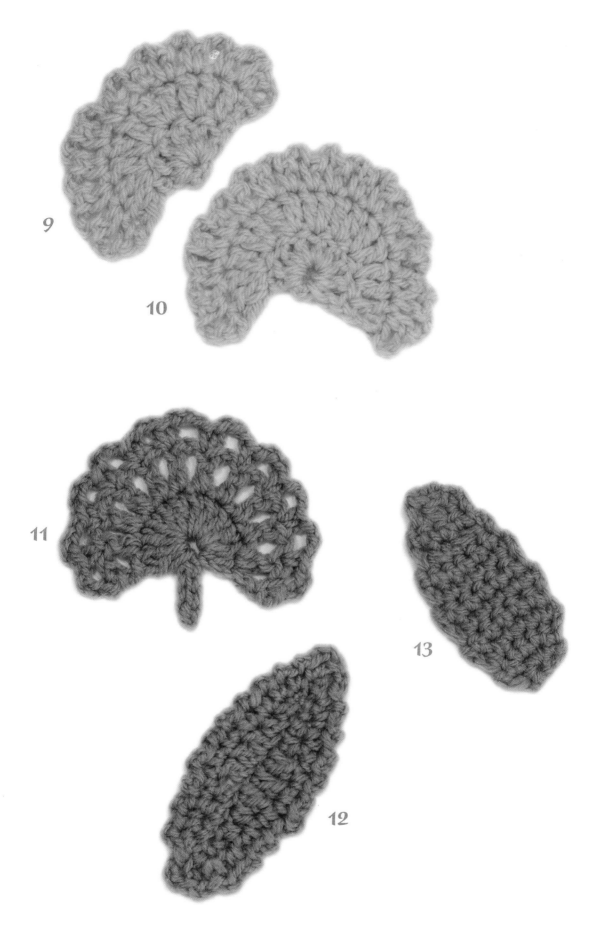

9

10

11

13

12

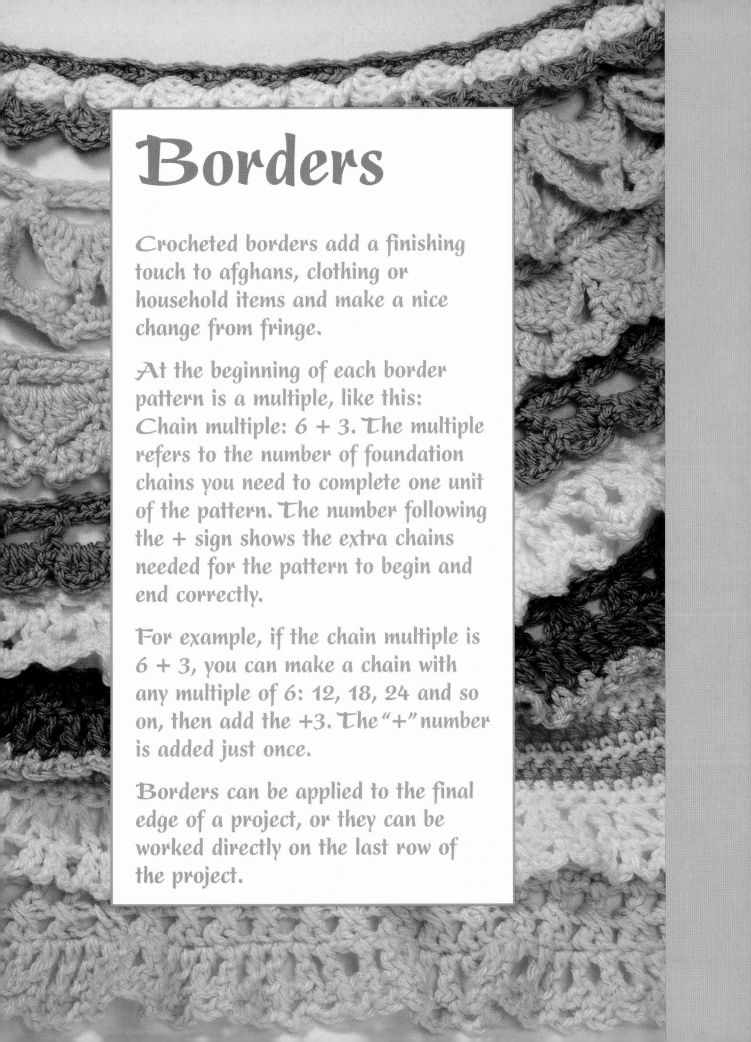

Borders

Crocheted borders add a finishing touch to afghans, clothing or household items and make a nice change from fringe.

At the beginning of each border pattern is a multiple, like this: Chain multiple: 6 + 3. The multiple refers to the number of foundation chains you need to complete one unit of the pattern. The number following the + sign shows the extra chains needed for the pattern to begin and end correctly.

For example, if the chain multiple is 6 + 3, you can make a chain with any multiple of 6: 12, 18, 24 and so on, then add the +3. The "+" number is added just once.

Borders can be applied to the final edge of a project, or they can be worked directly on the last row of the project.

Lilac Shells

Chain multiple: 5 + 2

Stitch Guide

Shell: In specified lp work (sc, hdc, 2 dc, tr, 2 dc, hdc, sc): shell made.

Instructions

Row 1 (right side): Sc in 2nd ch from hook and in each rem ch; ch 1, turn.

Row 2: Sc in first sc; *ch 4, skip 4 sc, sc in next sc; rep from * across; ch 1, turn.

Row 3: Sc in first sc; *work shell in next ch-4 lp, sc in next sc; rep from * across, ch 1, turn.

Row 4: Sc in first sc; *ch 4, sc in center tr of next shell, ch 4, sc in next sc between shells; rep from * across; ch 1, turn.

Row 5: Sc in first sc; *in next ch-4 lp work (sc, ch 3) twice, sc in same lp, sc in next sc; rep from * across. Finish off; weave in yarn ends.

Classy Points

Chain multiple: 10 + 6

Instructions

Row 1: Sc in 2nd ch from hook and in each rem ch, ch 3 (counts as a dc on following row), turn.

Row 2 (right side): Dc in next 4 sc; *ch 3, skip 2 sc, sc in next sc; ch 3, skip 2 sc, dc in next 5 sc; rep from * across, ch 1, turn.

Row 3: *Sc in next dc, (ch 4, skip next dc, sc in next dc) twice; in next sc work (tr, ch 4) twice, tr in same sc; rep from * across, ending last rep at with sc in next dc, ch 4, skip next dc, sc in next dc, ch 4, sk next dc, sc in top of turning ch-3; ch 1, turn.

Row 4: Sc in first dc; *(3 sc in next ch-4 sp, sc in next sc) twice; ** work 4 sc in next ch-4 sp, (sc, ch 4, sc) in next tr, 4 sc in next ch-4 sp, sc in next sc; rep from * across, ending last rep at **. Finish off; weave in yarn ends.

Cluster Shells

Chain multiple: 3 + 2

Two colors:
Color A (lavender)
Color B (white)

.Stitch Guide

Cluster (CL): *YO, insert hook in specified st and draw up a lp, YO and draw through 2 lps; rep from * in same st 2 times more, YO and draw through 4 lps: CL made.

Instructions

Work foundation chain with Color A.

Row 1: With Color A, sc in 2nd ch from hook and in each rem ch; ch 5 (counts as a dc and ch-2 sp on following row), turn.

Row 2 (right side): Skip next 2 sc, CL in next sc; *ch 2, skip 2 sc, CL in next sc; rep from * to last 3 sc, ch 2, skip next 2 sc, dc in last sc. Finish off Color A.

Row 3: Hold piece with right side facing; join Color B with sc in 3rd ch of turning ch-5; in rem ch sp of same turning ch work (sc, dc, tr, dc, sc), sc in next CL; *in next ch-2 sp work (sc, dc, tr, dc, sc),** sc in next CL; rep from * across, ending last rep at **; sc in last dc. Finish off; weave in yarn ends.

Simply Shells

Chain multiple: 4 + 2

Two Colors:

Color A (med blue)
Color B (white).

Stitch Guide

Shell: In specified st work (sc, ch 3, 3 dc): Shell made

Instructions

Work foundation chain with Color A.

Row 1(right side): With Color A, sc in 2nd ch from hook and in each rem ch, Finish off Color A.

Row 2 (right side): With right side facing, join Color B with sl st first sc at right, ch 1, work shell in same sc as joining;

*skip next 3 sc, shell in next sc; rep from * across. Finish off color B.

Row 3 (right side): With right side facing, join Color A in sp formed by first ch-3 at right, ch 1, work shell in same sp; *work shell in sp formed by next ch-3 sp; rep from * across, sc in last dc. Finish off; weave in yarn ends.

Ruffles and Ribbons

Chain multiple: 2

Two colors:

Color A (white)

Color B. (lavender)

Materials:

Length of ribbon to fit finished piece.

Instructions

Work foundation chain with Color A.

Row 1: With Color A, sc in 2nd ch from hook and in each rem ch; ch 4 (counts as a dc and ch-1 sp on following row), turn.

Row 2 (right side): *Skip next sc, dc in next sc, ch 1; rep from * across, ending last rep with dc in last sc. Finish off Color A.

Row 3 (right side): Hold piece with right side facing; join Color A with sc in 3rd ch of turning ch-4; *sc in next ch-1 sp, sc in next dc; rep from * across. Finish off Color A.

Row 4 (right side): With right side facing and starting ch at top, working in unused lps of foundation ch, join Color A with sl st in first lp at right, ch 3, dc in same lp; * ch 1, 2 dc in next unused lp; rep from * across. Finish off.

Row 5 (right side): Hold piece with right side facing and Row 4 at top. Join Color B with sc in 3rd ch of beg ch-3 on Row 4; sc in each dc and in each ch-1 sp across. Finish off; weave in yarn ends.

Weave ribbon through Row 2 as shown in photo.

Slanting Shells

Chain multiple: 3 + 2

Stitch Guide

Front Post Double Crochet (FPdc): YO; insert hook around post (vertical bar) of specified st from front to back to front and draw up a lp to height of a dc; YO and draw through 2 lps twice: FPdc made.

Instructions

Row 1 (right side): Sc in 2nd ch from hook and in each rem ch; ch 3 (counts as first dc on following row), turn.

Row 2: Dc in next sc and in each rem sc across; ch 1, turn.

Row 3: Sc in first dc; *sc in next dc, work 5 FPdc around post of same dc, dc in next 2 dc; rep from * across to last 2 sts, dc in next dc, sc in 3rd ch of turning ch-3. Finish off; weave in yarn ends.

Elegance

Chain multiple: 3 + 2

Instructions

Row 1 (right side): Sc in 2nd ch from hook and in each rem ch; ch 1, turn.

Row 2: Sc in first sc; *ch 3, skip 2 sc, sc in next sc; rep from * across; ch 1, turn.

Row 3: Sc in first sc; *ch 5, sc in next sc; rep from * across; ch 1, turn.

Row 4: Sc in first sc; *ch 7, sc in next sc; rep from * across; ch 1, turn.

Row 5: Sc in first sc; ch 5, dc in front of ch-7 lp of Row 3 and over ch-5 lp of Row 2; ch 5, sc in next sc; *ch 5, dc in front of next ch-7 and over ch-5 lp as

before, ch 5, sc in next sc; rep from * across; ch 1, turn.

Row 6: Sc in first sc; *ch 5, (dc, ch 3, dc) in next dc; ch 5, sc in next sc; rep from * across; ch 1, turn.

Row 7: *Work 5 sc in next ch-5 lp, (2dc, ch 3, 2 dc) in next ch-3 lp; 5 sc in next ch-5 lp, sc in next sc; rep from * across. Finish off; weave in yarn ends.

Fancy Shells

Chain multiple: 5 + 2

Stitch Guide

Shell: In specified lp work (sc, hdc, 2 dc, tr, ch 3, tr, 2 dc, hdc, sc): shell made

Instructions

Row 1 (right side): Sc in 2nd ch from hook and in each rem ch; ch 1, turn.

Row 2: Sc in first sc; *ch 8, skip 4 sc, sc in next sc; rep from * across; ch 1, turn.

Row 3: Sc in first sc; *work shell in next ch-8 lp, sc in next sc; rep from * across; ch 1, turn.

Row 4: Sc in first sc; *ch 6, in ch-3 sp of next shell work (dc, ch 3, dc); ch 6, sc in next sc; rep from * across; ch 1, turn.

Row 5: Sc in first sc; * work 8sc in next ch-6 sp, (sc, ch 3, sc) in ch-3 sp; work 8 sc in next ch-6 sp, sc in next sc; rep from * across. Finish off; weave in yarn ends.

Tone on Tone

Chain multiple: 3 + 2

Two colors:

Color A (med blue)

Color B (lt blue).

Instructions

Work foundation chain with Color A.

Row 1 (right side): Sc in 2nd ch from hook and in each rem ch; ch 3 (counts as first dc of following row), turn.

Row 2: Work 2 dc in base of ch; *skip next 2 sc, 3 dc in next sc; rep from * across; ch 4 (counts as a dc and ch-1 sp on following row), turn.

Row 3: Skip first dc, dc in next dc; *ch 1, dc in next dc; rep from * across to turning ch, ch 1, dc in 3rd ch of turning ch-3; finish off Color A.

Row 4: With right side facing, join Color B with sc in 3rd ch of ch-4; *ch 3, sc in next dc; rep from * across. Finish off; weave in yarn ends.

Pretty Peaks

Chain multiple: Any even number.

Stitch Guide

Shell: In specified sp work (dc, ch 3, dc): shell made

Instructions

Row 1: Sc in 2nd ch from hook and in each rem ch; ch 1, turn.

Row 2 (right side): Sc in first sc; *ch 3, skip next sc, sc in next sc; rep from * across; turn.

Row 3: Sl st into first ch-3 sp; ch 6 (counts as first dc and ch-3 sp of beg shell), dc in same ch-3 sp (beg shell made); *shell in next ch-3 sp; rep from * across; ch 1, turn.

Row 4: In ch-3 sp of first shell work (2 sc, ch 1, 2 sc); *sc between next 2 dc, in ch-3 sp of next shell work (2 sc, ch 3, 2 sc); rep from * across. Finish off; weave in yarn ends.

Crowned Shells

Chain multiple: 4 + 2

Stitch Guide

Shell: Work (hdc, dc, ch 1, dc, hdc) in specified lp: shell made

Instructions

Row 1: Sc in 2nd ch from hook and in each rem ch; ch 4 (counts as a dc and ch-1 sp on following row), turn.

Row 2 (right side): Skip next sc, dc in next sc; *ch 1, skip next sc, dc in next sc; rep from * across; ch 1, turn.

Row 3: Sc in first dc; *ch 5, skip next dc, sc in next dc; rep from * across, ending sc in 3rd ch of turning ch-4; ch 1, turn.

Row 4: Sc in first sc; *shell in next ch-5 lp, sc in next sc; rep from * across, ending last rep with sc in last dc; ch 6 (counts as a dc and ch-3 sp on following row), turn.

Row 5: Sc in ch-1 sp of first shell, ch 3, sc in next sc; *ch 3, sc in ch-1 sp of next shell, ch 3, sc in next sc; rep from * across. Finish off; weave in yarn ends.

Pointed Shells

Chain multiple: 8 + 3

Stitch Guide

Shell: Work (7 dc, ch 3, 7 dc) in specified lp: shell made

Instructions

Row 1 (right side): Sc in 2nd ch from hook and in each rem ch; ch 1, turn.

Row 2: Sc in first 5 sc; *ch 5, sc in next 8 sc; rep from * across to last 5 sc; ch 5, sc in last 5 sc; ch 1, turn.

Row 3: Sc in first sc, ch 5, sc in next sc; *shell in next ch-5 lp, skip next 3 sc, sc in next sc, ch 5, sc in next sc; rep from * across; finish off.

Row 4 (right side): With right side facing, join yarn with sl st in first ch-5 lp at right , ch 3 (counts as dc), 7 dc in same ch-5 lp; * ch 1; working behind next shell, sl st in back lps at bottom of center 2 dc (see fig), ch 1; work shell in next ch-5 lp ; rep from * across, ending last rep with 7 dc in last ch-5 lp, ch 3, sl st in same lp. Fnish off; weave in yarn ends.

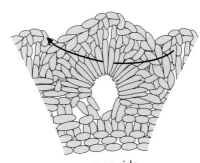

wrong side

Shaded Ruffles

Chain multiple: 4

Three colors:

Color A (dark blue)

Color B (med blue)

Color C (light blue)

Note: *A filet base is worked first, then ruffled rows are worked on this base.*

Instructions

FILET BASE

Work foundation ch with Color B.

Row 1 (right side): With Color B, sc in 2nd ch from hook and in each rem ch; ch 4 (counts as a dc and ch-1 sp on following rows), turn.

Row 2: Skip next sc, dc in next sc; *ch 1, skip next sc, dc in next sc; rep from * across; ch 4 (counts as a dc and ch-1 sp on following row), turn.

Row 3: Skip next ch, dc in next dc; *ch 1, sk next ch, dc in next dc; rep from * across, ending last rep with dc in 3rd ch of turning ch-4; ch 4, turn.

Row 4: Rep Row 3. At end of row, do not ch 4. Finish off.

RUFFLES

Working on filet base, you will work dc sts around the post (vertical bar) of dc sts on specified row, and around the ch-1 sps at top of specified row.

First Ruffle: With right side facing and foundation ch at right, join Color A with sl st around post of last dc worked on Row 2; ch 3 (counts as a dc), work 2 dc around post of same dc; *turn work so next ch-1 sp on Row 2 is at top and foundation ch is at bottom; work 3 dc in next ch-1 sp; turn work so that next dc on Row 2 is at top, and foundation chain is at left; work 3 dc around post of next dc; ** turn work so that next dc on Row 2 is at bottom and foundation ch is at right, work 3 dc around post of next dc; rep from * across, ending last rep at ** in turning ch sp. Finish off Color A.

Second Ruffle: With Color B, work as for First Ruffle around sts of Row 3, joining yarn in turning ch-4 sp and ending in last dc worked on Row 3.

Third Ruffle: With Color C, work as for First Ruffle around sts of Row 4. At end, weave in all yarn ends.

Lovely Loops

Chain multiple: Any number of chains

Instructions

Row 1 (right side): Sc in 2nd ch from hook and each rem ch; ch 3 (counts as a dc on following row), turn.

Row 2: Dc in next sc and in each rem sc; ch 5, turn.

Row 3: Sc in next dc; *ch 5, sc in next dc; rep from * across. Finish off; weave in yarn ends.

Pastel Parade

Chain multiple: Any even number

Three colors:

Color A (lt pink)

Color B (hot pink)

Color C (lime green)

Instructions

Work foundation chain with Color A.

Row 1 (right side): With Color A, sc in 2nd ch from hook and in each rem ch; ch 1, turn.

Row 2: Sc in each sc across, changing to Color B in last st; with Color B, ch 2 (counts as first hdc on following row), turn. Finish off Color A.

Row 3: With Color B, hdc next sc and in each rem sc. At end of row, finish off Color B.

Row 4: Hold piece with right side facing; join Color C with sc in top of ch-2 at right; sc in each hdc across, ch 1, turn.

Row 5: Sc in each sc across; at end of row, change to Color B in last st; ch 2 (counts as first hdc on following row), turn. Finish off Color C.

Row 6: With Color B, hdc in next sc and in each rem sc; at end of row, finish off Color B.

Row 7: Hold piece with right side facing; join Color A with sc in top of ch-2 at right; sc in each sc across; ch 1, turn.

Row 8: Sc in each sc across, ch 5 (counts as a dc and ch-2 sp on following row), turn.

Row 9: Dc in first sc; *skip next sc, work (dc, ch 2, dc) in next sc; rep from across; ch 1, turn.

Row 10: Sc in first dc; *ch 4, sc in next dc; rep from * across. Finish off; weave in all yarn ends.

Dainty Shells

Chain multiple: 3 + 2

Instructions

Row 1 (right side): Sc in 2nd ch from hook and in each rem ch; ch 5 (counts as a dc and ch-2 sp on following row), turn.

Row 2: Skip next 2 sc, dc in next sc; *ch 2, skip next 2 sc, dc in next sc; rep from * across; ch 1, turn.

Row 3: Sc in first dc; *in next ch-2 sp work (sc, dc, tr, dc, sc), sc in next dc; rep from * across to turning ch; in turning ch-5 lp work (sc, dc, tr, dc, sc), sc in 3rd ch of turning ch-5. Finish off; weave in yarn ends.

Over and Under

Chain multiple: 8 + 2

Two colors:

Color A (med green)

Color B (lt green).

Stitch Guide

Cluster (CL): (YO, insert hook in specified ch and draw up a lp to height of a dc, YO and draw through 2 lps on hook) 3 times in same ch, YO and draw through all 4 lps on hook: CL made.

Instructions

Work foundation chain with Color A.

Row 1 (right side): With Color A, sc in 2nd ch from hook and in each rem ch. Finish off.

Row 2 (right side): With right side facing, join Color A with sc in first sc at right on Row 1; (ch 4, CL in 4th ch from hook) 4 times, skip next 6 sc, sc in next 2 sc; leaving a long lp, remove hook from lp and drop Color A to front of work; working in front of Color A CLs, skip first 2 sc on Row 1, join Color B with sc in next sc, sc in next sc; (ch 4, CL in 4th ch from hook) 4 times; skip next 2 sc after last 2 sc worked in Color A, sc in next 2 sc; *leaving a long lp, remove hook from lp and drop Color B to front of work; **

return dropped lp of Color A to hook, working with Color A in front of CLs Color B, (ch 4, CL in 4th ch from hook) 4 times, skip next 2 sc after last 2 sc worked in Color B, sc in next 2 sc***; leaving a long lp, remove hook from lp and drop Color A to front of work; return dropped lp of Color B to hook; working with Color B in front of CLs of Color A, (ch 4, CL in 4th ch from hook) 4 times, skip next 2 sc after last 2 sc worked in Color A, sc in next 2 sc; rep from * across to last 4 sc. Finish off B; rep from ** to *** once. Finish off Color A; weave in yarn ends.

Elegant Edge

Chain multiple: 3 + 2

Instructions

Row 1: Sc in 2nd ch from hook and in each rem ch; ch 4 (counts as a dc and ch-1 sp on following row), turn.

Row 2 (right side): Skip next sc, dc in next sc; *ch 1, skip next sc, dc in next sc; rep from * across; ch 1, turn.

Row 3: Sc in first dc; *ch 5, skip next dc, sc in next dc; rep from * across, working last sc in 3rd ch of turning ch-4; ch 1, turn.

Row 4: Sc in first sc; *work 7 sc in next ch-5 lp, sc in next sc; rep from * across.

Finish off; weave in yarn ends.

Frankly Filet

Chain multiple: Any even number

Instructions

Row 1 (right side): Sc in 2nd ch from hook and in each rem ch; ch 4 (counts as a dc and ch-1 sp on following row), turn.

Row 2: Skip next sc, dc in next sc; * ch 1, skip next sc, dc in next sc; rep from * across; ch 5 (counts as a dc and ch-2 sp on following row), turn.

Row 3: Dc in next dc; *ch 2, dc in next dc; rep from * across to turning ch, dc in 3rd ch of turning ch-4; ch 6 (counts as a dc and ch-3 sp on following row), turn.

Row 4: Dc in next dc; *ch 3, dc in next dc; rep from * across to turning ch, ch 3,

dc in 3rd ch of turning ch-5; ch 1, turn.

Row 5: Sc in first dc; *in next ch-3 sp work (sc, ch 4, sc), sc in next dc; rep from * across to turning ch; in turning ch-6 lp work (sc, ch 4, sc), sc in 3rd ch of turning ch. Finish off; weave in yarn ends.

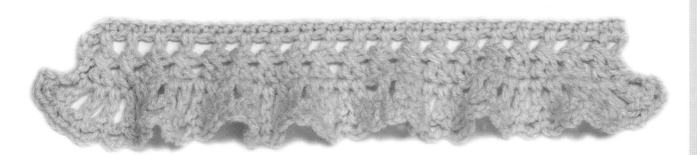

Crossed Doubles

Chain multiple: Any even number

Instructions

Row 1 (right side): Sc in 2nd ch from hook and in each rem ch; ch 4 (counts as a dc and ch-1 sp on following row), turn.

Row 2 (right side): Skip next sc, dc in next sc; *ch 1, skip next sc, dc in next sc; rep from * across; ch 3 (counts as a dc on following row), turn.

Row 3: *Skip next ch-1 sp, dc in next dc, dc in skipped ch-1 sp; rep from * across, ending last rep with dc in 3rd ch of turning ch-4; ch 4 (counts as a dc and ch-1 sp on following row), turn.

Row 4: *Dc in next dc, ch 1; rep from * across, ending last rep with dc in 3rd ch of turning ch; ch 1, turn.

Row 5: Sc in first dc; *ch 3, sc in next dc; rep from * across to turning ch, ch 3, sc in 3rd ch of turning ch-4. Finish off; weave in yarn ends.

Bands

Bands are similar to borders, but instead of being worked onto the final edge of a project, they are sewn onto the project. Bands have a decorative edge on both top and bottom, rather than on just the bottom as in borders. They are wonderful accents for clothing and towels, or as a shelf accent.

At the beginning of each band pattern is a multiple, like this: Chain multiple: 6 + 3. The multiple refers to the number of foundation chains you need to complete one unit of the pattern. The number following the + sign shows the extra chains needed for the pattern to begin and end correctly.

For example, if the chain multiple is 6 + 3, you can make a chain with any multiple of 6: 12, 18, 24, and so on, then add the +3. The "+" number is added just once.

Rickrack

Note: *Pattern is not worked on a foundation chain base.*

Instructions

Ch 4.

Row 1: Work 3 dc in 4th ch from hook; ch 3, turn.

Row 2: Work 3 dc in first dc; ch 3, turn, leaving rem dc unworked.

Repeat Row 2 for desired length. Finish off; weave in yarn ends.

Scarlet Ribbons

Chain multiple: Any even number

Two colors:

Color A (white)

Color B (red)

Additional Materials:

Ribbon of desired length.

Note: *Row 2 can be adjusted to fit various sizes of ribbon. For wider ribbon, work Row 2 with dc or tr instead of hdc. If working Row 2 with dc, ch 1 more at end of Row 1; If working Row 2 with tr, ch 2 more at end of Row 1.*

Instructions

Work foundation chain with Color A

Row 1 (right side): With Color A, sc in 2nd ch from hook and in each rem ch; ch 3 (counts as hdc and ch-1 sp on following row), turn.

Row 2: Skip next sc; *hdc in next sc, ch 1, sk next sc; rep from * across, ending last rep with hdc in last sc; ch 1, turn.

Row 3: Sc in first hdc; sc in each ch-1 sp and in each hdc across, ending last rep with sc in turning ch-3 sp, sc in 2nd ch of turning ch-3. Finish off.

Row 4 (right side): With right side facing, join Color A with sl st in first sc at right; ch 3, work 2 dc in base of ch; *work 2 dc in next sc, 3 dc in next sc; rep from * across. Finish off.

Row 5 (right side): With right side facing, join Color B with sc in 3rd ch of beg ch-3 on Row 4;

*ch 1, sc in next dc; rep from * across. Finish off Color B.

Row 6 (right side): Hold piece with right side facing and foundation chain at top. Working in unused lps of foundation ch, join Color A with sl st in first lp at right; ch 3, work 2 dc in base of ch-3; *work 2 dc in next lp, work 3 dc in next lp; rep from * across. Finish off Color A.

Row 7(right side): With right side facing, join Color B with sc in top of turning ch at right of Row 6; * ch 1, sc in next dc; rep from * across. Finish off; weave in yarn ends.

Finishing

Weave ribbon through mesh formed in Row 2. Sew ribbon ends securely in place.

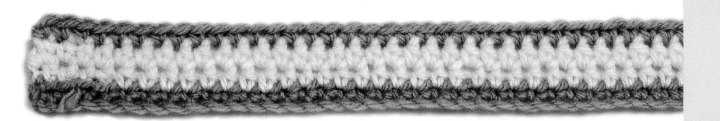

Tri-Color Ribbon

Chain multiple: Any number

Three colors:

Color A (green)

Color B (pink)

Color C (yellow)

Instructions

Work foundation chain with Color A

Row 1 (right side): With Color A, sc in 2nd ch from hook and in each rem ch, changing to Color B in last st; with Color B, ch 1, turn. Finish off Color A.

Row 2: With Color B, sc in first sc and in each sc across, changing to Color C in last st; with Color C, ch 1, turn. Finish off Color B.

Row 3: With Color C, sc in first sc and in each sc across, changing to Color A in last st; with color A, ch 1, turn.

Row 4: With Color A, sc in first sc and in each sc across. Finish off Color A; weave in yarn ends.

Wave the Flag

Chain multiple: 11 + 10

Three colors:

Color A (red)

Color B (white)

Color C (blue)

Instructions

Work foundation chain with Color A.

Row 1 (right side): With Color A, sc in 2nd ch from hook and in each of next 3 chs; *work 3 sc in next ch, sc in next 4 chs, skip next 2 chs, sc in next 4 chs; rep from * across to last 5 chs; work 3 sc in next ch, sc in last 4 chs. Finish off Color A.

Row 2 (right side): Hold piece with right side facing; join Color B with sc in first sc at right; skip next sc, sc in next 3 sc; *work 3 sc in next sc (center sc of 3-sc group on last row), sc in next 4 sc, skip next 2 sc, sc in next 4 sc; rep from * across to last 6 sc; work 3 sc in next sc (center sc of 3-sc group on last row), sc in next 3 sc, skip next sc, sc in last sc. Finish off Color B.

Row 3 (right side): With Color C, work same as Row 2. Finish off Color C; weave in all yarn ends.

Ruffled Row

Chain multiple: 4 + 2

Two colors:
Color A (red)
Color B (white)

Stitch Guide

Shell: Work 5 dc in specified st: shell made.

Instructions

Work foundation chain with Color A **Row 1 (right side):** With Color A, sc in 2nd ch from hook; *skip next ch, shell in next ch, skip next ch, sc in next ch; rep from * across. Finish off Color A.

Row 2 (right side): With right side facing, join Color B with sc in first sc at right; * (ch 3, sc in next dc of shell) 5 times, ch 3, sc in next sc; rep from * across. Finish off Color B.

Row 3 (right side): Hold piece with right side facing and foundation ch at top. Working in unused lps of foundation ch, join Color A with sc in first lp at right, skip next lp, shell in next lp (same ch in which shell was worked on Row 1) skip next lp , sc in next lp; rep from * across. Finish off Color A.

Row 4 (right side): With right side facing, join Color B with sc in first sc at right of Row 3; *(ch 3, sc in next dc of shell) 5 times, ch 3, sc in next sc; rep from * across. Finish off Color B. Weave in yarn ends.

Rainbow

Chain multiple: Any even number

Seven colors:
Color A (red)
Color B (orange)
Color C (bright yellow)
Color D (green)
Color E (blue)
Color F (lavender)
Color G (pale yellow)

Instructions

Work foundation chain with Color A.

Row 1 (right side): Sc in 2nd ch from hook and in each rem ch. Finish off Color A.

Row 2 (right side): Hold piece with right side facing; join Color B with sc in first sc at right; sc in each sc across. Finish off Color B.

Rnds 3 through 6: Rep Row 2 four times more, once each with Color C, Color D, Color E and Color F, in that order.

Top Border: Hold piece with right side facing and last row worked at top. Join Color G with sc in first sc at right; *ch 3, skip next sc, sc in next sc; rep from * across. Finish off.

Bottom Border: Hold piece with right side facing and foundation chain at top. Working in unused lps of foundation ch, join Color G with sc in first ch at right; *ch 3, skip next ch, sc in next ch; rep from * across. Finish off; weave in yarn ends.

Springtime

Chain multiple: 4 + 2

Four colors:
Color A (cream)
Color B (green)
Color C (pink)
Color D (yellow)

Additional Materials:

Large-eyed tapestry needle.

Stitch Guide

Shell: In specified st work (sc, hdc, dc, hdc, sc): shell made

Instructions

Work foundation chain with Color A.

Row 1 (right side): With Color A, sc in 2nd ch from hook and in each rem ch; ch 1, turn.

Row 2: Sc in first sc and each sc across, ch 1, turn.

Rows 3 through 5: Rep Row 2.

Row 6: Sc in each sc. Finish off.

Top Edging: With right side facing and Row 6 at top, join Color B with sc in first sc at right of Row 6; *skip next sc, shell in next sc, skip next sc, sc in next sc; rep from * across. Finish off Color B.

Bottom Edging: Hold piece with right side facing and foundation chain at top. Working in unused lps of foundation chain, join Color A with sc in first lp at right; *skip next lp. work shell in next lp, work skip next lp, sc in next lp; rep from * across. Finish off Color B. Weave in yarn ends.

EMBROIDERY

On right side, mark for flower centers placed about 3" apart. Thread Color C into tapestry needle and following diagrams, work five lazy daisy sts around each center mark. With Color D, work a French Knot in center of each flower. With Color B, work straight sts for leaves placed between each flower as shown in photo.

Linked Clusters

Note: *Pattern is not worked on a foundation chain base.*

Stitch Guide

Cluster (CL): *YO, insert hook in 4th ch from hook and draw up a lp to height of a dc; YO and draw through 2 lps; rep from * two times more in same ch, YO and draw through 4 lps: CL made.

Instructions

Row 1: *Ch 4, work CL in 4th ch from hook; rep from * for desired length of band. Finish off; weave in yarn ends.

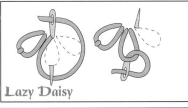

Lazy Daisy

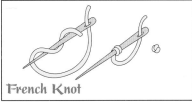

French Knot

Straight Stitch

Topsy Turvy

Chain multiple: 4 + 2

Two colors:
Color A (rose)
Color B (pink)

Stitch Guide

Shell: In specified st work
(dc, ch 1) twice, dc in same st:
shell made

Instructions

Work foundation chain with
Color A

Row 1 (right side): With Color
A, sc in 2nd ch from hook;
*skip next ch, work shell in next
ch, skip next ch, sc in next ch;
rep from * across. Finish off
Color A.

Row 2 (right side): With right
side facing join Color B with sc
in first sc at right; *sc in first dc
of next shell, sc in next ch-1 sp,
work 3 sc in next dc, sc in next
ch-1 sp, sc in next dc, sc in next
sc; rep from * across. Finish off
Color B.

Row 3 (right side): With right
side facing, hold piece with
foundation ch at top; working
in unused lps of foundation ch,
join Color B with sc in first lp at
right *skip next lp, work shell in
next lp (same ch in which shell
was previously worked on Row
1), skip next lp, sc in next lp;
rep from * across. Finish off
Color B.

Row 4 (right side): With right
side facing, join Color A with sc
in first sc at right; *sc in first dc
of next shell, sc in next ch-1 sp,
work 3 sc in next dc, sc in ch-1
sp, sc in next dc, sc in next sc;
rep from * across. Finish off
Color A; weave in yarn ends.

Crossed Stitches

Chain multiple: 6 + 2

Two colors:
Color A (lt blue)
Color B (med blue)

Instructions

Work foundation chain with
Color A.

Row 1 (right side): With Color
A, sc in 2nd ch from hook and
in each rem ch; ch 3 (counts as
a dc on following row), turn.

Row 2: *Skip next sc, dc in next
sc, dc in skipped sc, dc in next
sc; rep from * across; ch 1, turn.

Row 3: Sc in first dc and in
each dc across. Finish off Color
A.

Row 4: With right side facing,
join Color B with sc in first sc at
right of Row 3; sc in first sc and
in each sc across, ch 1, turn.

Row 5: Sc in first sc; *ch 3, skip
next sc, sc in next sc; rep from *
across. Finish off.

Row 6: Hold piece with right
side facing and foundation ch
at top. Working in unused lps of
foundation ch, join Color B
with sc in first lp at right; sc in
next lp and in each lp across,
ch 1, turn.

Row 7: Sc in first sc; *ch 3, skip
next sc, sc in next sc; rep from *
across. Finish off; weave in yarn

Snow Balls

Chain multiple: 4 + 2

Two colors:
Color A (white)
Color B (blue)

Stitch Guide

Popcorn Stitch (Pst): Work 4 dc in specified st. Drop lp from hook, insert hook from front to back in top of first dc worked; insert hook in dropped lp and draw through, ch 1 to tighten st (Pst made)

Note: *Final ch 1 of Pst does not count as a ch-1 sp on row following.*

Instructions

Work foundation chain with Color A

Row 1: With Color A, sc in 2nd ch from hook and in each rem ch; ch 4 (counts as a dc and ch-1 sp on following row), turn.

Row 2 (right side): *Skip next sc, Pst in next sc, ch 1 (in addition to final ch-1 of Pst), skip next sc, dc in next sc, ** ch 1; rep from * across, ending last rep at **; ch 1, turn.

Row 3: Sc in first dc; *sc in next ch-1 sp, sc in next Pst,**; sc in next ch-1 sp, sc in next dc; rep from * across, ending last rep at **; sc in turning ch-4 sp, sc in 3rd ch of turning ch-4. Finish off Color A.

Row 4: Hold piece with right side facing and Row 3 at top; join Color B with sc in first sc at right; *ch 3, sc in next sc; rep from * across. Finish off Color B.

Row 5: Hold piece with right side facing and foundation ch at top; working in unused lps of foundation ch, join Color B with sc in first lp at right; *ch 3, sc in next lp; rep from * across. Finish off; weave in yarn ends.

Lilac Shells

Chain multiple: 4 + 2

Two colors:
Color A (purple)
Color B (lilac)

Stitch Guide

Shell: Work 5 dc in specified st: shell made

Instructions

Work foundation chain with Color A

Row 1 (right side): With Color A, sc in 2nd ch from hook and in each rem ch. Finish off Color A.

Row 2 (right side): With right side facing, join Color B with sc in first sc at right; *skip next sc, shell in next sc, skip next sc, sc in next sc; rep from * across.

Finish off Color B.

Row 3 (right side): With right side facing, turn work so foundation ch is at top. Working in unused lps of foundation ch, join Color B with sc in first lp at right. *skip next lp, shell in next lp, skip next lp, sc in next lp; rep from * across. Finish off; weave in yarn ends.

53

Braids & Cords

You'll find many uses for braids and cords in your crochet work. Braids make lovely textured accents for clothing, decorating home furnishings items from pillows to lampshades and waste baskets or as a curtain tieback. You'll find dozens of uses for these versatile braids. Cords are used for drawstrings or ties, or for straps on bathing suits or tube tops. Although a simple chain can be used as a cord, it won't have much substance and will twist. Try our versions instead.

Braids

This collection of braids is truly international: it includes braids from Russia, the Ukraine, Belgium, and Romania. Several of these braids are traditionally used in ethnic laces. Braids are quick and easy to make. We've shown ours worked in size 3 crochet cotton, but they can be crocheted in any weight yarn you prefer. Smooth yarns make the braid details stand out.

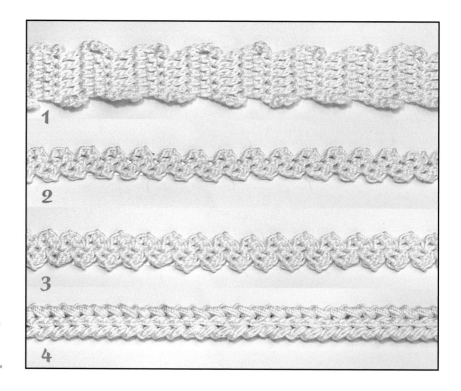

Braid 1

Instructions

Ch 10.

Row 1: Dc in 6th ch from hook and in each rem ch across: 5 dc; ch 5, turn.

Row 2: Dc in each dc; ch 5, turn.

Repeat Row 2 for pattern. At end of last row, do not ch or turn. Finish off.

Braid 2

Instructions

Ch 2.

Row 1: 3 sc in 2nd ch from hook: 3 sc; ch 1, turn.

Row 2: Sc in first sc, 2 sc in front lp of next sc: 3 sc; ch 1, turn, leaving rem sc unworked.

Repeat Row 2 until braid is desired length. At end of last row, do not ch or turn. Finish off.

Braid 3

Instructions

Ch 3.

Row 1: Sc in 2nd ch from hook, 3 sc in next ch: 4 sc; ch 1, turn.

Row 2: Sc in first sc, 3 sc in next sc: 4 sc; ch 1, turn, leaving rem 2 sc unworked.

Repeat Row 2 until braid is desired length. At end of last row, do not ch or turn. Finish off.

Braid 4

Stitch Guide

Cluster (CL): Insert hook in specified st or sp and draw up a lp, (YO, insert hook in same specified st or sp and draw up a lp) 2 times; YO and draw through all 6 lps on hook: CL made.

Instructions

Ch 3.

Row 1: CL in 3rd ch from hook; ch 1, turn.

Row 2: CL in same ch as first CL; ch 1, turn.

Row 3: CL in center of CL 2 rows below, inserting hook after first front lp of CL; ch 1, turn.

Repeat Row 3 until braid is desired length. Finish off.

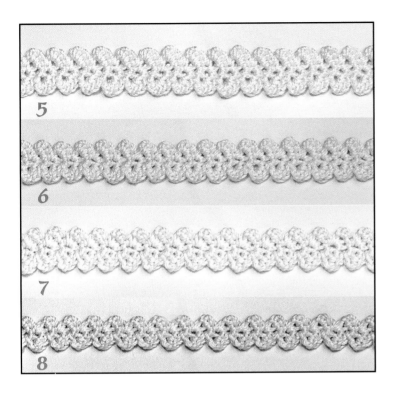

Braid 5

Instructions

Ch 4.

Row 1: Work 3 sc in 2nd ch from hook, 2 sc in next ch, sc in next ch: 6 sc; ch 1, turn.

Row 2: Work 3 sc in first sc, 2 sc in next sc, sc in next sc; ch 1, turn, leaving last 3 sc unworked.

Repeat Row 2 until braid is desired length. At end of last row, do not ch or turn. Finish off.

Braid 6

Instructions

Ch 3.

Row 1: Work 3 sc in 2nd ch from hook, 2 sc in next ch: 5 sc; ch 1, turn.

Row 2: Work 3 sc in first sc, 2 sc in next sc; ch 1, turn, leaving last 3 sc unworked.

Repeat Row 2 until braid is desired length. At end of last row, do not ch or turn. Finish off.

Braid 7

Instructions

Ch 4.

Row 1: Sc in 2nd ch from hook, sc in next ch, 3 sc in last ch: 5 sc; ch 1, turn.

Row 2: Sc in first 2 sc, 3 sc in next sc; ch 1, turn, leaving last 2 sc unworked.

Repeat Row 2 until braid is desired length. At end of last row, do not ch or turn. Finish off.

Braid 8

Instructions

Ch 4.

Row 1: Sc in 2nd ch from hook, skip next ch, 3 sc in last ch: 4 sc; ch 1, turn.

Row 2: Sc in first sc, 3 sc in next sc; ch 1, turn, leaving last 2 sc unworked.

Repeat Row 2 until braid is desired length. At end of last row, do not ch or turn. Finish off.

Braid 9

Instructions

Ch 3; join with sl st to form a ring.

Row 1: Work 5 sc in ring: 5 sc; ch 1, turn.

Row 2: Work 5 sc in back lp of first sc, sl st in both lps of same sc; ch 1, turn.

Repeat Row 2 until braid is desired length. At end of last row, do not ch or turn. Finish off.

Braid 10

Instructions

Ch 4.

Row 1: Work 4 dc in 4th ch from hook, ch 3, sl st in ch at base of 4 dc; ch 3, turn.

Row 2: Work (4 dc, ch 3, sl st) in ch-3 sp; ch 3, turn.

Repeat Row 2 until braid is desired length. At end of last row, do not ch or turn. Finish off.

Braid 11

Instructions

Ch 5.

Row 1: Work (3 dc, ch 2, 3 dc) in 5th ch from hook; ch 5, turn.

Row 2: Work (3 dc, ch 2, 3 dc) in ch-2 sp; ch 5, turn.

Repeat Row 2 until braid is desired length. At end of last row, do not ch or turn. Finish off.

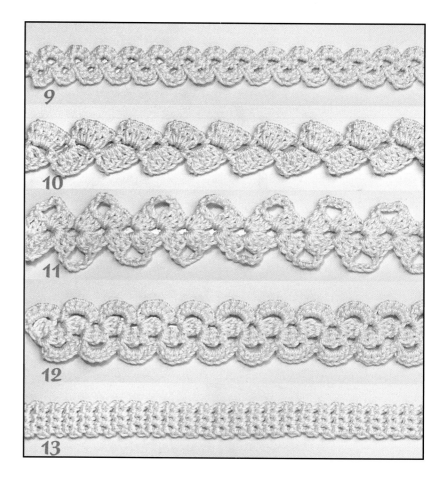

Braid 12

Stitch Guide

Cluster (CL): *(YO, insert hook in specified st or sp and draw up a lp to height of a dc, YO and draw through 2 lps on hook); rep from * 2 times more in same st or sp, YO and draw through all 4 lps on hook: CL made.

Instructions

Ch 3.

Row 1: (CL, ch 3, sl st) in 3rd ch from hook; ch 1, turn.

Row 2: Work 6 sc in first ch-3 sp, ch 3, (CL, ch 3, sc) in sp formed by skipped chs at beg of Row 1; ch 1, turn.

Row 3: Work 6 sc in first ch-3 sp, ch 1, (CL, ch 3, sc) in next ch-3 sp; ch 1, turn.

Repeat Row 3 until braid is desired length.

Last Row: Work 6 sc in first ch-3 sp. Finish off.

Braid 13

Instructions

Ch 4.

Row 1: Sc in 2nd ch from hook and in next 2 chs: 3 sc; ch 1, turn.

Row 2: Sc in each sc across; ch 1, turn.

Repeat Row 2 until braid is desired length. At end of last row, do not ch or turn. Finish off.

Braid 14

Instructions

Ch 3.

Row 1: Work (5 dc, ch 3, sc) in 3rd ch from hook; ch 4, turn.

Row 2: (Sc, hdc, 3 dc, tr, ch 3, sc) in ch-3 sp; ch 4, turn.

Repeat Row 2 until braid is desired length. At end of last row, do not ch or turn.
Finish off.

Braid 15

Instructions

Ch 8.

Row 1: Sc in 2nd ch from hook and in next 2 chs, 3 sc in next ch, sc in next 3 chs: 9 sc; ch 1, turn.

Row 2: Skip first sc, sc in back lp of next 3 sc, 3 sc in back lp of next sc, sc in back lp of next 3 sc; ch 1, turn, leaving last sc unworked.

Repeat Row 2 until braid is desired length. At end of last row, do not ch or turn.
Finish off.

Braid 16

Instructions

Ch 8.

Row 1: Dc in 4th ch from hook and in next 4 chs: 5 dc; ch 3 (counts as first dc on next row now and throughout), turn.

Row 2: Work 3 dc in first dc, (2 dc in next dc) 3 times, dc in last dc: 11 dc; ch 3, turn.

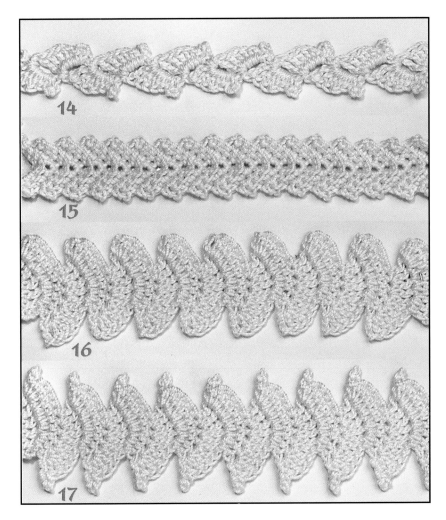

Row 3: Work 3 dc in first dc, (2 dc in next dc) 3 times, dc in next dc; ch 3, turn, leaving last 6 dc unworked.

Repeat Row 3 until braid is desired length. At end of last row, do not ch or turn.
Finish off.

Braid 17

Instructions

Ch 8.

Row 1: Dc in 4th ch from hook and in next 4 chs: 5 dc; ch 4, turn.

Row 2: Sl st in 3rd ch from hook, 3 dc in first dc, (2 dc in next dc) 3 times, dc in last dc: 10 dc; ch 4, turn.

Row 3: Sl st in 3rd ch from hook, 3 dc in first dc, (2 dc in next dc) 3 times, dc in next dc; ch 4, turn, leaving last 5 dc unworked.

Repeat Row 3 until braid is desired length. At end of last row, do not ch or turn.
Finish off.

Cords

Although we've shown our cords worked in size 3 crochet cotton, you'll want to try them in a variety of types and sizes of yarns. Just remember not to use drawstrings in garments for babies or young children because of the danger of strangulation. When used as drawstrings, each end is usually knotted.

1 Slip Stitch Cord

Instructions

Chain the desired length, plus a little extra; sl st in 2nd ch from hook and in each rem ch; finish off. When working the sl sts, be sure to draw each st completely up onto the working part of the hook.

2 Single Crochet Cord

Instructions

Chain the desired length, plus a little extra; sc in 2nd ch from hook and in each rem ch; finish off.

3 Half Double Crochet Cord

Instructions

Chain the desired length, plus a little extra; hdc in 3rd ch from hook and in each rem ch; finish off.

4 Parallel Chain

Instructions

Place loose slip knot on hook, insert hook in bottom of slip knot (see fig) and draw up a lp; *gently remove one lp from hook and hold base of removed lp so it does not pull out or twist, YO and draw through lp on hook, place removed lp back on hook, YO and draw through one lp on hook; rep from * until chain is desired length.
Note: *This cord is stretchy!*

5 Romanian Cord

Instructions

Working loosely, ch 2, sc in top lp of 2nd ch from hook (Step 1), turn work 90 degrees clockwise (Step 2), sc in 2 lps on left (Steps 3, 4 and 5); *turn work 90 degrees clockwise (Step 6), sc in 2 lps on left that were formed by sc before last sc made (Step 6); rep from * until cord is desired length (Step 7).

6 Textured Cord

Instructions

Ch 3, pull up lp on hook about $1/4$", insert hook in 2nd ch from hook and draw up a $1/4$" lp, insert hook in 3rd ch from hook and draw up a $1/4$" lp, YO and draw through all 3 elongated lps on hook; pull up lp on hook about $1/4$", turn work clockwise (to the left), insert hook under top 2 strands and draw up a $1/4$" lp, insert hook in next lp to left of last 2 strands and draw up a $1/4$" lp, YO and draw through all 3 elongated lps on hook; *pull up lp on hook about $1/4$", turn work clockwise (to the left), insert hook under top 2 strands and draw up a $1/4$" lp, insert hook under next 3 lps to left of last 2 strands and draw up a $1/4$" lp, YO and draw through all 3 elongated lps on hook; rep from * until cord is desired length.

7 Round Cord

Instructions

Ch 5.

Rnd 1: Sc in 5th ch from hook and in each rem ch around: 5 sc. Do not join.

Rnd 2: Sc in first sc and in each rem sc around. Do not join.

Rep Rnd 2 until cord is desired length. Sl st in next sc; finish off.

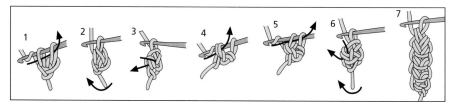

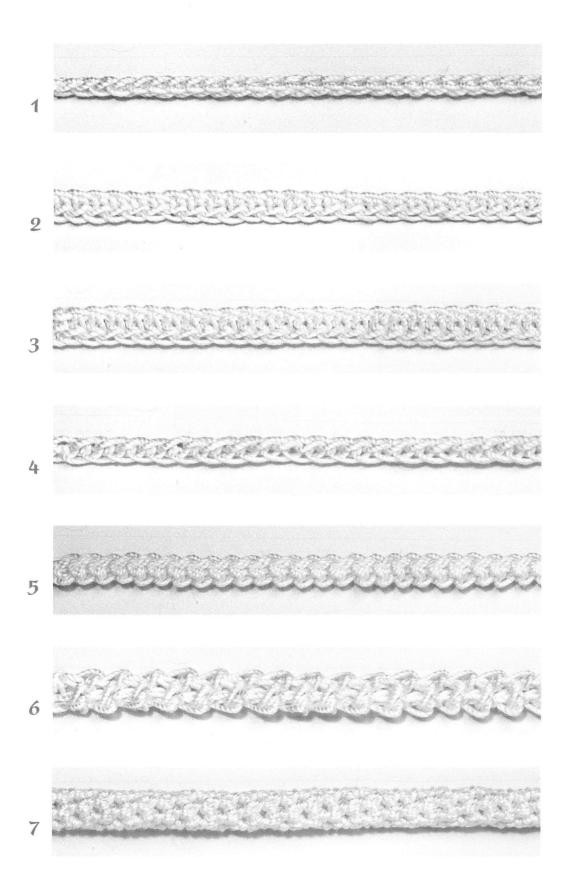

Motifs & Shapes

Motifs come in a variety of shapes and styles, and are excellent accents for many projects. Our motifs range from stars to heraldic symbols. We have also included instructions for basic classic shapes—circles and squares, triangles, pentagons and hexagons.

Lazy Circle

Two colors:

Color A (yellow)

Color B (pink)

Instructions

With Color A, ch 6, join with a sl st to form a ring.

Rnd 1: Ch 3 (counts as a dc), work 23 dc in ring; join with sl st to top of beg ch-3: 24 dc. Finish off Color A.

Rnd 2: Join Color B with sc in any dc; *ch 3, skip next dc, sc in next dc; rep from * around, ending last rep with ch 3; do not join.

Rnd 3: *Sc in next ch-3 lp, ch 4; rep from * around, do not join.

Rnd 4: *Sc in next ch-4 lp, ch 5; rep from * around, ending last rep with sc in beg ch-5 lp. Finish off; weave in yarn ends.

Be Mine

Two colors:

Color A (red)

Color B (white)

Instructions

Row 1: With Color A, ch 4 (counts as a dc), work 2 dc in 4th ch from hook: 3 dc; ch 3 (counts as first dc of following row), turn.

Row 2: Work 3 dc in next dc, dc in next dc; ch 3, turn: 5 dc.

Row 3: Dc in base of ch, dc in next dc, 3 dc in next dc, dc in next dc, 2 dc in last dc: 9 dc; turn.

Row 4: Sl st in first dc; skip next dc, in next dc work 5 dc; skip next dc, sl st in next dc; skip next dc, 5 dc in next dc, skip next dc, sl st in last dc. Do not turn.

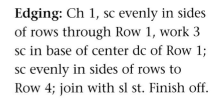

Edging: Ch 1, sc evenly in sides of rows through Row 1, work 3 sc in base of center dc of Row 1; sc evenly in sides of rows to Row 4; join with sl st. Finish off.

Lacy Border: Join Color B with sl st in center sl st of Row 4; *ch 3, sc in next st; rep from * around, join in beg sl st. Finish off; weave in yarn ends.

Shield

Two Colors:

Color A (green)

Color B (gold)

Instructions

With Color A, ch 6; join with sl st to form a ring.

Rnd 1: Ch 3 (counts as a dc), in ring work 2 dc, (ch 3, 3 dc) twice, ch 3, join in 3rd ch of beg ch-3. Finish off Color A.

Rnd 2: Join Color B in any ch-3 sp; ch 3 (counts as a dc) in same sp work (2 dc, ch 3, 3 dc) for corner; *dc in each of next 3 dc, in next ch-3 sp work (3 dc, ch 3, 3 dc) for corner; rep from * once more, dc in each of last 3 dc. Finish off Color B.

Rnd 3: Join Color A in first dc of any corner group; ch 3, dc in next 2 dc; *working over Rnd 2 and into ch-3 sp of Rnd 2, work (2 tr, ch 3, 2 tr); dc in each rem 3 dc of corner group; dc in next 6 dc; rep from * 2 times more, dc in last 6 dc. Finish off; weave in yarn ends.

Octagon

Three colors:

Color A (dk blue)

Color B (yellow)

Color C (med blue)

Stitch Guide

Shell: Work 7 dc in specified st: shell made.

Instructions

With Color A, ch 4, join with sl st to form a ring.

Rnd 1: Sl st in ring; ch 3 (counts as a dc), 15 dc in ring; join in top of beg ch-3: 16 dc. Finish off Color A.

Rnd 2: Join Color B with sc in any dc; *skip next dc, shell in next dc, skip next dc, sc in next dc; rep from * around, ending last rep with sl st in beg sc. Finish off Color B.

Rnd 3: Join Color C with sc in 4th dc of any shell; *ch 3, in next sc work (2 tr, ch 3, 2 tr); ch 3, sc in 4th dc of next shell; rep from * around, ending last rep with join with sc in beg sc.

Rnd 4: Ch 3, sc in same sc; *3 sc in next ch-3 sp, sc in each of next 2 tr, in next ch-3 sp work (sc, ch 3, sc), sc in each of next 2 tr; work 3 sc in next ch-3 sp, in next sc work (2 sc, ch 3, 2 sc) rep from * around, ending last rep with 3 dc in last ch-3 sp, join in beg sc. Finish off Color C; weave in yarn ends.

Golden Wheel

Three colors:

Color A (dk green)

Color B (gold)

Color C (med green)

Stitch Guide

Shell: In specified lp work
(3 dc, ch 3, 3 dc): shell made.

Instructions

With Color A, ch 4, join with sl st to form a ring.

Rnd 1: Ch 1, work 8 sc in ring; join with sl st in beg sc. Finish off Color A.

Rnd 2: Join Color B with sc in any sc, sc in same st; work 2 sc in each rem sc around: 16 sc; join in beg sc.

Rnd 3: *Ch 10, sl st in next 2 sc; rep from * around, ending last rep with join in beg sl st. Finish off Color B: 8 ch-10 lps.

Rnd 4: Join Color C with sl st in any ch-10 lp; ch 3, in same lp work (2 dc, ch 3, 3 dc); work shell in each rem ch-10 lp around; join in 3rd ch of beg ch-3. Finish off Color C; weave in yarn ends.

Picot Points

Stitch Guide

Picot: Ch 3, sl st in first ch made: picot made.

Shell: In specified lp work (sc, 4 dc, work picot, 4 dc, sc): shell made.

Instructions

Ch 6, join with sl st to form a ring.

Rnd 1: Sl st in ring, ch 3 (counts as a dc), work 2 dc in ring, work picot; *work 3 dc in ring, work picot; rep from * 4 times more; join with sl st in top of beg ch-3: 18 dc and 6 picots.

Rnd 2: Sc in next dc; *ch 8, skip next dc, next picot and next dc, sc in next dc; rep from * 5 times more join with sl st in beg sc: 6 ch-8 lps.

Rnd 3: *Work shell in next ch-8 lp; rep from * around, join in beg sc 8 shells. Finish off; weave in yarn ends.

Falling Star

Two colors:

Color A (lime green)

Color B (red)

Instructions

With Color A, ch 4, join with sl st to form a ring.

Rnd 1: Ch 1, work 12 sc in ring; join in beg sc. Finish off Color A.

Rnd 2: Join Color B with sc in any sc; *ch 5; sl st in 2nd ch from hook, sc in next ch hdc in next ch, dc in next ch, skip next sc on Rnd 1, sc in next sc; rep from * around, ending last rep with join with sl st in beg sc. Finish off Color B; weave in yarn ends.

Gold Star

Stitch Guide

Shell: In specified sp work (3 dc, ch 3, 3 dc): shell made.

Instructions

Ch 6, join to form a ring.

Rnd 1: Ch 3, work 2 dc in ring; (ch 3, 3 dc in ring) 4 times, ch 3, join in 3rd ch of beg ch-3.

Rnd 2: Sl st in each of next 2 dc, sl st into next ch-3 sp; in same sp work (ch 3, 2 dc, ch 3, 3 dc); *ch 1, shell in next ch-3 sp; rep from * around, ending last rep with ch 1, join with sc in top of beg ch-3.

Rnd 3: Sc in next 2 dc; *3 sc in ch-3 sp, sc in next 3 dc, dc in ch-1 sp, sc in next 3 dc; rep from * around, ending last rep with sc in last ch-1 sp, join in beg sc. Finish off; weave in yarn ends.

69

Daisy Wheel

Two colors:

Color A (yellow)

Color B (pink).

Stitch Guide

Puff Stitch (Pst): *YO, insert hook in ring and draw up a lp to height of a dc; rep from * 2 times more, YO and draw through all 7 lps on hook: Pst made.

Instructions

With Color A, ch 6, join with sl st to form a ring.

Rnd 1: Sl st in ring, ch 3; (Pst in ring, ch 3) 8 times, skip beg ch-3, join with sc in top of first Pst.

Rnd 2: *Work 3 sc in next ch-3 sp, sc in top of next Pst; rep from * around, ending last rep with 3 sc in last ch-3 sp; join in beg sc. Finish off Color A.

Rnd 3: Join Color B in sc above any Pst; *2 dc in next sc, dc in next sc, 2 dc in next sc, sc in next sc; rep from * around ending last rep with join in beg sc. Finish off Color B; weave in yarn ends.

Quadrafoil

Two colors:

Color A (lt brown)

Color B (med brown)

Instructions

With Color A, ch 10; join with sl st to form a ring.

Rnd 1: Ch 3 (counts as a dc), work 23 dc in ring, join with sl st in top of beg ch-3: 24 dc; finish off Color A.

Rnd 2: Join Color B with sc in any dc, sc in each of next 2 dc, work (sc, ch 7, sc) in next dc; *sc in next 5 dc, work (sc, ch 7, sc) in next dc; rep from * around, ending last rep with sc in last 2 dc; join with sc in beg sc.

Rnd 3: *In next ch-7 lp work (7 dc, ch 3, 7 dc), skip next 2 sc, ** sc in next sc, skip next 2 sc; rep from * around, ending last rep at **; join with sl st in beg sc. Finish off; weave in yarn ends.

Rising Sun

Instructions

Rnd 1: Ch 4 (counts as a dc), work 11 dc in 4th ch from hook; join with sc in 4th ch of beg ch-4: 12 dc.

Rnd 2: Sc in same dc; work 2 sc in each rem dc around: 24 sc; join with sc in beg sc.

Rnd 3: *Ch 8, sl st in 2nd ch from hook, sc in next ch, hdc in next ch, dc in next 4 chs: point made; skip next 2 dc of Rnd 2, sc in next dc; rep from * around, join in beg sc: 8 points made. Finish off; weave in yarn ends. Lightly steam if needed so points will lie flat.

Peacock's Eye

Four colors:

Color A (deep blue)

Color B (lime green)

Color C (tan)

Color D (lt green)

Instructions

Rnd 1: With Color A, ch 4 (counts as first dc of rnd); work 11 dc in 4th ch from hook; join with sl st in top of beg ch-4: 12 dc. Finish off Color A.

Rnd 2: Join Color B in any dc; ch 3 (counts as a dc), dc in same dc; work 2 dc in each rem dc around; join in top of beg ch-3. Finish off Color B.

Rnd 3: Join Color C with sc in any dc, work another sc in same st; work 2 sc in each dc until 6 sts rem; 2 hdc in each of next 2 sts, in next st work (dc, tr), in next st work (tr, dc), in each of next 2 sts work 2 hdc; join with sl st in beg sc of rnd. Finish off Color C.

Rnd 4: Join Color D with sc in same sc as last sl st made; sc in each sc around to dc, work 2 sc in each of next 2 dc, sc in each rem st; join with sl st in beg sc.

Rnd 5: *Ch 2, sl st in next st; rep from * around, ending last rep with ch 2, join in beg sl st. Finish off Color D; weave in yarn ends. Lightly steam piece if needed to keep work flat.

Shapes

Crochet motifs can be made in just about any shape. Here are five classic shapes that you may find useful.

Note: *All are made with three colors:*
Color A (yellow), Color B (blue) and Color C (white)

---

1 Square

Instructions

With Color A, ch 4, join with sl st to form a ring.

Rnd 1: Ch 3 (counts as a dc), 2 dc in ring, (ch 3, 3 dc in ring) 3 times, ch 3, join with sl st in top of beg ch-3: 4 ch-3 sps. Finish off Color A.

Rnd 2: Join Color B with sl st in any ch-3 sp; in same sp work (ch 3, 2 dc, ch 3, 3 dc): corner made; * ch 1, in next ch-3 sp work (3 dc, ch 3, 3 dc): corner made; rep from * two times more; ch 1, join in top of beg ch-3. Finish off Color B.

Rnd 3: Join Color C with sl st in any ch-3 corner sp; in same sp work (ch 3, 2 dc, ch 3, 3 dc); * ch 1, work 3 dc in next ch-1 sp for side, ch 1, in next corner ch-3 sp work (3 dc, ch 3, 3 dc); rep from * two times more, ch 1, work 3 dc in last ch-1 sp, ch 1, join with sl st in top of beg ch-3.

Rnd 4: Ch 1, sc in same st as joining; sc in each dc and in each ch-1 sp around, working 3 sc in each ch-3 sp; join in beg sc. Finish off; weave in yarn ends.

2 Triangle

Instructions

With Color A, ch 4, join with sl st to form a ring.

Rnd 1: Ch 3 (counts as a dc), 2 dc in ring; (ch 3, 3 dc in ring) two times, ch 3, join with sl st in top of beg ch-3: 3 ch-3 sps. Finish off Color A.

Rnd 2: Join Color B with sl st in any ch-3 sp; in same sp work (ch 3, 2 dc, ch 3, 3 dc): corner made; * ch 1, in next ch-3 sp work (3 dc, ch 3, 3 dc); rep from * once, ch 1, join with sl st in top of beg ch-3. Finish off Color B.

Rnd 3: Join Color C with sl st in any ch-3 corner sp; in same sp work (ch 3, 2 dc, ch 3, 3 dc); * ch 1, work 3 dc for side in next ch-1 sp; in next ch-3 sp work (3 dc, ch 3, 3 dc); rep from * once, ch 1, 3 dc in next ch-1 sp; join with sl st in top of beg ch-3.

Rnd 4: Ch 1, sc in joining; sc in each dc and in each ch-1 sp around, working 3 sc in each corner ch-3 sp. Finish off; weave in yarn ends.

3 Circle

Instructions

With Color A, ch 4 (counts as a dc).

Rnd 1: Work 11 dc in 4th ch from hook, join in 4th ch of beg ch-4: 12 dc; finish off Color A.

Rnd 2: Join Color B with sl st in any dc; ch 3 (counts as a dc), dc in joining; work 2 dc in each dc around: 24 dc; join. Finish off Color B.

Rnd 3: Join Color C with sl st in any dc; ch 3 (counts as a dc) *2 dc in next dc, dc in next dc; rep from * around: 36 dc; join in top of beg ch 3.

Rnd 4: Ch 1, sc in joining; sc in each dc around, join in beg sc. Finish off; weave in yarn ends.

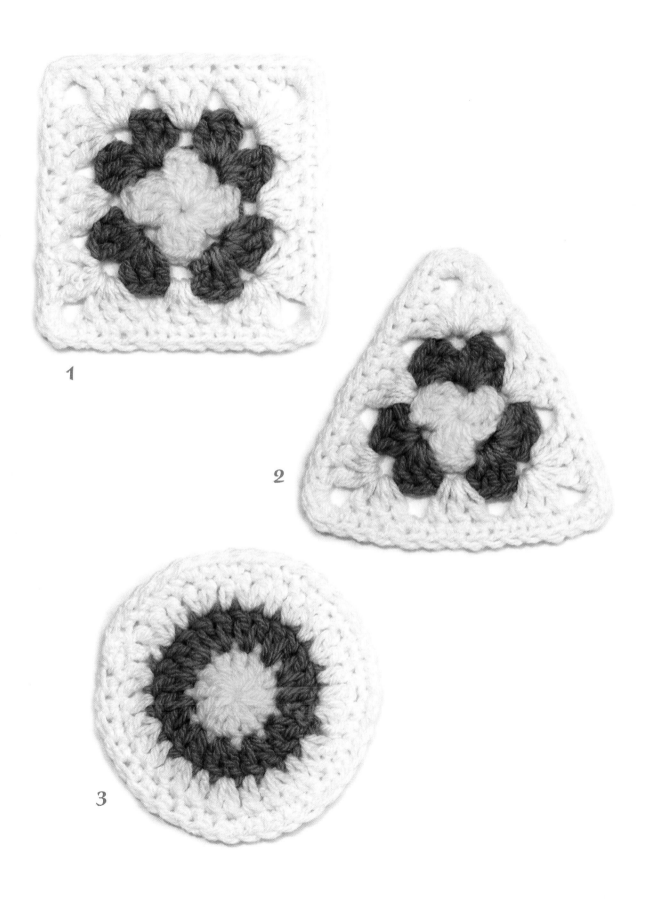

1

2

3

4 Pentagon

Instructions

With Color A, ch 5; join with sl st to form a ring.

Rnd 1: Ch 3 (counts as a dc), work 2 dc in ring; (ch 3, work 3 dc in ring) 4 times, ch 3, join in top of beg ch-3: 5 ch-3 sps. Finish off Color A.

Rnd 2: Join Color B with sl st in any ch-3 sp; in same sp work (ch 3, 2 dc, ch 3, 3 dc): corner made; *ch 1, in next ch-3 sp work (3 dc, ch 3, 3 dc): corner made; rep from * 3 times more; ch 1, join in top of beg ch-3. Finish off Color B.

Rnd 3: Join Color C with sl st in any ch-3 corner sp; in same sp work (ch 3, 2 dc, ch 3, 3 dc); *ch 1, work 3 dc in next ch-1 sp for side; ch 1, in next corner ch-3 sp work (3 dc, ch 3, 3 dc); *rep from * 3 times more, ch 1, work 3 dc in next ch-1 sp, ch 1, join with sl st in top of beg ch-3.

Rnd 4: Ch 1, sc in joining; sc in each dc and in each ch-1 sp around, working 3 sc in each ch-3 sp. Finish off; weave in yarn ends.

5 Hexagon

Instructions

With Color A, ch 6; join with sl st to form a ring.

Rnd 1: Ch 3 (counts as a dc), work 2 dc in ring; (ch 3, work 3 dc in ring) 5 times, ch 3, join in top of beg ch-3. Finish off Color A.

Rnd 2: Join Color B with sl st in any ch-3 sp; in same sp work (ch 3, 2 dc, ch 3, 3 dc): corner made; *ch 1, in next ch-3 sp work (3 dc, ch 3, 3 dc): corner made; rep from * 4 times more; ch 1, join in top of beg ch-3; Finish off Color B.

Rnd 3: Join Color C with sl st in any ch-3 corner sp; in same sp work (ch 3, 2 dc, ch 3, 3 dc); *ch 1, work 3 dc in next ch-1 sp for side, ch 1, in next corner ch-3 sp work (3 dc, ch 3, 3 dc); rep from * 4 times more, ch 1, work 3 dc in last ch-1 sp, ch 1, join with sl st in top of beg ch-3.

Rnd 4: Ch 1, sc in same st as joining; sc in each dc and in each ch-1 sp around, working 3 sc in each ch-3 sp; join in beg sc. Finish off; weave in yarn ends.

Final Touches

Favorite final touches include fringes, tassels, curliques, beads and buttons. All are easy and fun to crochet and make a project very special. Tassels make great gifts, and often are used in home décor to tie on a drawer handle or a door knob. Final touches put the "wow" factor in your projects.

Tassels

You can mix a variety of materials in a tassel, including metallic or furry yarns. Here's how to make the basic version.

Basic Tassel

Cut a piece of cardboard 1/2" longer than the length desired for the tassel.

Place a 12" piece of yarn or cord across the top for the tie and wind yarn around the cardboard and over the tie until you have the desired thickness.

Draw the tie up tightly and knot securely.

Cut yarn at bottom of cardboard and slide off the cardboard.

Cut another 12" piece of yarn or cord and wrap tightly about an inch below the top of tassel. Wrap several times, then tie a secure knot. Trim ends of cord and bottom of tassel as desired.

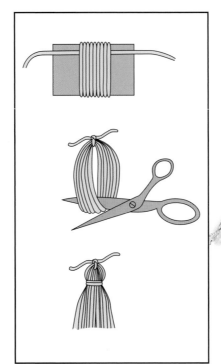

Wild and Crazy Tassel

Size: 10" long plus hanging lp

Materials

20" long strands of assorted scrap yarns for tassel skirt

1 oz sport or DK weight yarn for crocheted tassel top

Size E (3.5 mm) crochet hook (or size required for gauge)

1 yd gold cord for hanging loop and tying

3 beads, 3/8" diameter

Craft glue or hot glue

Large-eyed tapestry needle

Instructions

TASSEL TOP

Gauge: 6 sc = 1"

Ch 2.

Rnd 1: Work 6 sc in 2nd ch from hook; do not join; mark beg of rnds.

Rnd 2: Work 2 sc in each sc around, do not join: 12 dc.

Rnd 3: *Sc in next sc, 2 sc in next sc; rep from * around: 18 sc; do not join.

Rnds 4 through 9: Sc in each sc.

Rnd 10: *Ch 4, sc in next sc; rep from * around, join with sl st in beg sc. Finish off; weave in yarn ends.

Cut a piece of same yarn 12" long; thread yarn into a tapestry needle and weave in and out between sts of Rnd 6. Leave ends loose until top is put onto the tassel skirt.

TASSEL SKIRT

Following instructions for Basic Tassel on page 80, cut a piece of cardboard 11" wide, or 1" longer than desired finished length of tassel. Wrap yarn around cardboard to desired thickness. Cut a Thread a 14" piece of cord and fold in half; thread cut ends into tapestry needle and slide under all yarn strands at top, draw up tightly, knot securely. Move cord lp to top of piece to serve as hanger later. Cut yarn at opposite side and remove cardboard. Set piece aside.

FINISHING

Thread cord lp into tapestry needle and draw lp and skirt up into Top piece, bringing Cord lp through center of Top. Draw up loose ends of yarn on top tightly and knot, tie in a bow.

Draw cord lp through 3 beads and lightly glue in place. Trim yarn ends as desired.

Beads 'n Bows

Designed by Susan Lowman

Size: 8" long plus hanging loop

Materials

Aunt Lydia's Fashion Crochet Thread, size 3

    10 yds Natural #226

    25 yds Warm Teal #65

Size E (3.5 mm) crochet hook (or size required for gauge)

Size 6 glass beads, #16002 Midnight and #16602 Frosted Ice by Mill Hill

12" of heavy metallic braid (#32), #005 Black by Kreinik

44" of medium metallic braid (#16), #044 Confetti Blue by Kreinik

Small amount of fiberfill or cotton balls

Bead threader or dental floss threader

Fabric glue

Gauge

Rnds 1 through 5 = 3/4" high x 3/4" diameter

Special Stitches

Sc decrease (sc dec): Insert hook in first specified st and draw up a lp, insert hook in 2nd specified st and draw up a lp, YO and draw through all 3 lps on hook: sc dec made.

To join with sc: Place slip knot on hook, insert hook in specified st and draw up a lp, YO and draw through 2 lps on hook.

Instructions

Starting at top with natural, ch 4; join with sl st to form a ring.

Rnd 1: Ch 1, 8 sc in ring: 8 sc; join with sl st in first sc.

Rnd 2: Ch 1, sc in same st as joining, 2 sc in next st, (sc in next st, 2 sc in next st) 3 times: 12 sc; join as before.

Rnds 3 through 5: Ch 1, sc in same st as joining and in each st around; join.

Cut 8" length of teal for hanging loop. Fold in half and tie overhand knot near cut ends. Insert folded end from inside through hole in top. Glue knot to inside top.

Stuff top section firmly with small amount of fiberfill or cotton ball.

Rnd 6: Ch 1, sc dec in same st as joining and in next st, (sc dec in next 2 sts) 5 times: 6 sc; join with sl st in first sc dec.

Rnd 7: Rep Rnd 3: 6 sc.

Rnd 8: Ch 1, 2 sc in same st as joining, (2 sc in next st) 5 times: 12 sc; join.

Rnd 9: Ch 1, sc in same st as joining and in next st, 2 sc in next st, (sc in next 2 sts, 2 sc in next st) 3 times: 16 sc; join.

Rnd 10: Rep Rnd 3. Finish off; weave in ends.

Rnd 11: Join teal with sc in first st, sc in next st and in each st around; join with sl st in first sc.

Rnd 12: Rep Rnd 3. Finish off; weave in ends.

Rnd 13: With natural, rep Rnd 11.

Rnd 14: Rep Rnd 3.

Rnd 15: Ch 1, sc in same st as joining and in next st, sc dec in next 2 sts, (sc in next 2 sts, sc dec in next 2 sts) 3 times: 12 sc; join.

Stuff middle section firmly with small amount of fiberfill or cotton balls.

Rnds 16 through 19: Rep Rnds 6 through 9.

Rnds 20 and 21: Rep Rnd 3 two times more.

Stuff bottom section firmly with small amount of fiberfill or cotton balls.

Rnd 22: Ch 1, working all sc dec sts in back lps throughout rnd, sc dec in same st as joining and in next st, (sc dec in next 2 sts) 7 times: 8 sc; join with sl st in first sc dec.

Rnd 23: Ch 1, sc dec in same st as joining and in next st, (sc dec in next 2 sts) 3 times: 4 sc; join as before. Finish off; weave in ends.

FRINGES

With bead threader or dental floss threader, string 80 beads onto teal thread as follows: [1 midnight, 1 frosted ice] 40 times. Holding tassel with Rnd 1 at top, join teal with sl st in front lp of last sc on Rnd 21, *ch 10, pull a bead up to hook, ch 1 to anchor bead; ch 15, pull 3 beads up to hook, ch 1 to anchor beads; ch 15, pull a bead up to hook, ch 1 to anchor bead; ch 10, making sure ch is not twisted, sl st in front lp of next sc on Rnd 21; ch 15, pull a bead up to hook, ch 1 to anchor bead; ch 10, pull 3 beads up to hook, ch 1 to anchor beads; ch 10, pull a bead up to hook, ch 1 to anchor bead, ch 15;making sure ch is not twisted, sl st in front lp of next sc on Rnd 21; rep from * 7 times more, ending with sl st in joining sl st on Rnd 21; join with sl st in first sl st. Finish off; weave in ends.

BOWS

Cut two 12″ strands of blue metallic braid and one 12″ strand of black metallic braid. Tie all 3 strands together in a bow around tassel between middle and bottom sections. Cut two 10″ strands of blue metallic braid. Tie both strands together in a bow around tassel between top and middle sections.

Tassel with Elegance

Designed by Susan Lowman

Size: 7" long plus hanging loop

Materials

Aunt Lydia's Fashion Crochet Thread, size 3

    35 yds Bridal White #926

    25 yds Tangerine #325

Size E (3.5 mm) crochet hook (or size required for gauge)

Size 6 glass beads, #16602 Frosted Ice and #16606 Brilliant Bronze by Mill Hill

90" of 1/16" ribbon, #9192 Light Peach by Kreinik

Small amount of fiberfill or cotton balls

Bead threader or dental floss threader

Fabric glue

Tapestry needle

Gauge

Rnds 1 through 5 = 3/4" high x 1" diameter

Special Stitches

Sc decrease (sc dec): Insert hook in first specified st and draw up a lp, insert hook in 2nd specified st and draw up a lp, YO and draw through all 3 lps on hook: sc dec made.

To join with sc:
Place slip knot on hook, insert hook in specified st and draw up a lp, YO and draw through 2 lps on hook.

Shell: Work (4 hdc, ch 3, 4 hdc) in specified st or sp: shell made.

Picot: Ch 4, sl st in top of last sc made: picot made.

Instructions

Starting at top with white, ch 4; join with sl st to form a ring.

Rnd 1: Ch 1, 8 sc in ring: 8 sc; join with sl st in first sc.

Rnd 2: Ch 1, 2 sc in same st as joining, (2 sc in next st) 7 times: 16 sc; join as before.

Rnds 3 through 10: Ch 1, working in back lps throughout rnds, sc in same st as joining and in each st around; join with sl st in both lps of first sc.

Cut 8" length of white for hanging loop. Fold in half and tie overhand knot near cut ends. Insert folded end from inside through hole in top. Glue knot to inside top.

Stuff top section firmly with small amount of fiberfill or cot-

ton balls.

Rnd 11: Ch 1, working in back lps through rnd, sc dec in same st as joining and in next st, (sc dec in next 2 sts) 7 times: 8 sc; join with sl st in first sc dec.

Rnd 12: Ch 1, sc dec in same st as joining and in next st, (sc dec in next 2 sts])3 times: 4 sc; join as before. Finish off; weave in ends.

TOP DECORATION

Rnd 1: Holding top section with Rnd 1 at bottom, join white with sc in front lp of first sc on Rnd 2, sc in front lp of each sc around: 16 sc; join with sl st in

84

first sc.

Rnd 2: Ch 1, sc in same st as joining and in next 2 sts; *ch 4, sc in next 4 sts; rep from * 2 times more; ch 4, sc in last st: 16 sc and 4 ch-4 lps; join as before.

Rnd 3: Ch 1, sc in same st as joining; *ch 4, sc in next st, shell in next ch-4 lp**; skip next st, sc in next st; rep from * 2 times more, then rep from * to ** once: 4 shells and 4 ch-4 lps; join. Remove lp from hook.

Rnd 4: Working behind last rnd, join orange with sc in center of any ch-4 lp on rnd before last (where shell on last rnd was worked); *picot, shell in next ch-4 lp**; working behind next shell, sc in center of next ch-4 lp on rnd before last (where shell on last rnd was worked); rep from * 2 times more, then rep from * to ** once; join. Remove lp from hook.

Rnd 5: Replace white lp onto hook, ch 2; *working behind next shell, sc in center of next ch-4 lp on rnd before last (where shell on last rnd was worked), picot, shell in ch-4 lp of next picot on last rnd; rep from * 3 times more; join. Remove lp from hook.

Rnd 6: Replace orange lp onto hook, ch 2; rep Rnd 5 from * to end. Do not remove lp from hook. Finish off; weave in ends.

Rnd 7: Replace white lp onto hook, ch 2; *working behind next shell, sc in center of next ch-4 lp on rnd before last (where shell on last rnd was worked), shell in ch-4 lp of next picot on last rnd; rep from * 3 times more; join. Finish off; weave in ends.

FRINGES
String 24 white beads on white thread and 24 brown beads on orange thread. Holding top section with Rnd 1 at bottom, join white with sl st in front lp of first sc on Rnd 10; *(ch 35, pull 3 beads up to hook, ch 1 to anchor beads; ch 35, skip next sc on Rnd 10, sl st in front lp of next sc on Rnd 10) 8 times, ending with sl st in first sl st. Finish off; weave in ends*. Fold white ch lps down over top section. Holding top section with Rnd 1 at bottom, join orange with sl st in front lp of last sc on Rnd 10, rep from * to *. Cut eight 9" strands of ribbon. Fold ribbon in half. Insert hook in front lp of any sc on Rnd 9, draw folded end through lp and rest of ribbon through fold. Pull ends of ribbon to secure. Repeat with each ribbon in front lp of every other sc on Rnd 9.

BOW
Cut 18" strand of ribbon. Using tapestry needle, weave ribbon in and out of every other st on Rnd 2 of Top Decoration. Tie in a bow. String 3 beads onto ends of bow and tie 2 knots close to ends of ribbon to secure.

Bead & Button Covers

Crocheting covers for wooden beads is easy and fun, and the beads make trendy accents for everything from jewelry to ceiling fan pulls. Any size wooden bead can be used, as long as it has a hole completely through it. The covered beads can be used for buttons too, by adding a short chain at the end to serve as a shank.

We have used embroidery floss for our beads because of the availability of such a wide variety of colors, but crochet cotton in any size can also be used. Have fun making them with stripes, or use the ombre or variegated threads. Metallics add a fun touch. If you want to use the beads for a necklace, placing a few glass beads between the crocheted ones adds sophistication.

We've given you instructions for three different sizes of wood beads, which are available at most craft stores.

Materials

Six-strand embroidery floss or size 10 crochet cotton in your choice of colors.

Round wood beads with center hole, 15mm, 16 mm or 20 mm

Stitch marker

Size 5 (1.9mm) steel crochet hook (or size required for gauge)

Gauge

16 sc = 1"

16 sc rows = 1"

Stitch Guide

Sc 2 tog decrease (sc 2 tog): Draw up a lp in each of next 2 sts, YO and draw through all 3 lps on hook: decrease made.

Instructions

FOR 15 MM BEAD:
Ch 2.

Rnd 1: Work 6 sc in 2nd ch from hook; do not join, mark beg of rnds.

Rnd 2: Work 2 sc in each sc: 12 sc.

Rnd 3: (Sc in each of next 3 sc, 2 sc in next sc) 3 times: 15 sc.

Rnds 4 through 7: Sc in each sc.

Rnd 8: (Sc in next 3 sc, sc 2 tog) 3 times: 12 sc.

Place bead in crocheted cup, making sure bead hole is standing vertically in center of cup.

Rnd 9: (Sc 2 tog) 6 times: 6 sc rem. Finish off, leaving a long thread end. Thread end into a tapestry needle and weave through rem 6 sts; draw up tightly to close, fasten securely.

For button shank: With matching thread join yarn with sl st in closure; ch 5, sl st in 2nd ch from hook and in each rem ch; join in beg sl st. Finish off, weave in end.

FOR 16 MM BEAD:
Ch 2.

Rnd 1: 6 sc in 2nd ch from hook; do not join, mark beg of rnds.

Rnd 2: Work 2 sc in each sc: 12 sc.

Rnd 3: (Sc in each of next 2 sc, 2 sc in next sc) 4 times: 16 sc.

Rnds 4 through 8: Sc in each sc.

Rnd 9: (Sc in each of next 2 sc, sc 2 tog) 4 times: 12 sc.

Place bead in crocheted cup, making sure bead hole is standing vertically in center of cup.

Rnd 10: (Sc 2 tog) 6 times: 6 sc rem. Finish off, leaving a long thread end. Thread end into a tapestry needle and weave through rem 6 sts; draw up tightly to close, fasten securely.

For button shank: With matching thread join yarn with sl st in closure; ch 5, sl st in 2nd ch from hook and in each rem ch. Finish off, weave in end.

FOR 20 MM BEAD:
Ch 2.

Rnd 1: Work 7 sc in 2nd ch from hook; do not join, mark beg of rnds.

Rnd 2: Work 2 sc in each sc: 14 sc.

Rnd 3: (Sc in next 3 sc, 2 sc in next sc) 3 times, sc in last 2 sc: 17 sc.

Rnds 4 through 9: Sc in each sc.

Rnd 10: (Sc in next 3 sc, sc 2 tog) 3 times, sc in last 2 sc: 14 sc.

Place bead in crocheted cup, making sure bead hole is placed vertically in center of cup.

Rnd 11: (Sc 2 tog) 7 times: 7 sc.

Finish off, leaving a long end. Thread end into tapestry needle and weave through rem 7 sc; draw up tightly to close, and secure. Weave in ends.

For button shank: With matching thread join yarn with sl st in closure; ch 5, sl st in 2nd ch from hook and in each rem ch; join in beg sl st. Finish off; weave in ends.

Curlicues

These curls are quick and easy to make, and are fun to use on children's clothing, or as a substitute for fringe. They are often used to make doll hair.

They can be made with any yarn, and whatever length you desire.

1

CURL 1
Instructions

Make a chain of desired length.

Row 1: Work 3 sc in 2nd ch from hook; work 3 sc in each rem ch. Finish off; weave in yarn ends.

CURL 2
Instructions

Make a chain of desired length.

Row 1: Work 2 dc in 4th ch from hook; work 3 dc in each rem ch. Finish off; weave in yarn ends.

2

CURL 3
Instructions

Make a chain of desired length with first color.

Row 1: Work 2 dc in 4th ch from hook; work 3 dc in each rem ch. Finish off.

Row 2: Starting at top of curl, join contrast yarn with sc in first dc; work sc in each dc across. Finish off; weave in yarn ends.

3

Fringe

We most often think of fringe as a finish for afghans, but it actually has many uses. Fringe looks great on pillows and cushions, on rugs, and on children's clothing. Fringe made with crochet cotton can be used on curtains or table runners.

Most patterns state how long to cut the yarn, and how many strands to use in each knot. Generally, cut the strands twice the length you want the finished fringe to be, plus about 2" extra for the knots. Triple knot, or other more elaborate knotting styles, may require 3" or 4" extra.

An easy way to make fringe is to find a book close to the length you need, and wind the yarn around that. After you have wound and cut a few fringe pieces, make one or two knots to see if you are happy with the length.

SINGLE KNOT FRINGE
This is the fringe most often used on afghans. Although any number of strands can be used, 4 strands is usually the minimum.

Hold the specified number of strands for one knot of fringe together, and then fold in half.

Hold the project with the right side facing you. Using a crochet hook, draw the folded ends through the space or stitch from right to wrong side.

Pull the loose ends through the folded section.

Draw the knot up firmly.

SPAGHETTI FRINGE (not shown)
This is made with just one strand in the knot, and the knots are usually spaced very close together.

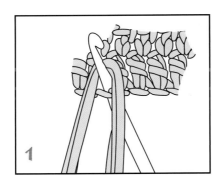
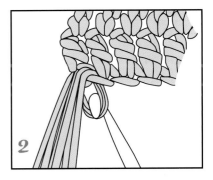

DOUBLE KNOT FRINGE

First work a complete row of Single Knot Fringe, then using half the strands from one knot and half the strands from the next knot, tie a row of knots about 1¹/₂" below the first row.

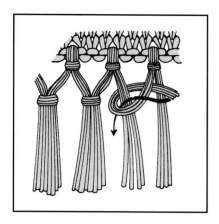

TRIPLE KNOT FRINGE

First work Double Knot Fringe, then add one more row of knots below.

SLANTED TRIPLE KNOT

Similar to Triple Knot, the knots are tied by jumping over one more group of strands before tying the knot.

CHAIN FRINGE WITH SHELL TOPPER

This is a good fringe to use when a yarn frays easily.

Row 1: To prepare for this, with the right side of the piece facing you, work one row of single crochet evenly across the edge to be fringed. Finish off.

Row 2: With right side facing, join the yarn in the back lp only of the first sc at right. *Ch 24 (or desired length), sc in back lp only of next sc; rep across, being sure to work in back lps only of each stitch. Finish off.

Shell Topper (optional)

Row 1: With right side facing, working in the front lps only of Row 2, join yarn (we used a yarn that contrasted with the fringe) with sc in front lp of

first sc at right; *skip next sc, in next sc work shell of (3 dc, ch 3, sl st in base of ch just worked, 3 dc); skip next sc, sc in next sc; rep from * across. Finish off; weave in yarn ends.

A Refresher Course in Crochet

SLIP STITCH

To begin, make a slip knot (sometimes called a slip loop) on the hook, leaving a 6" tail of yarn (**Fig 1**).

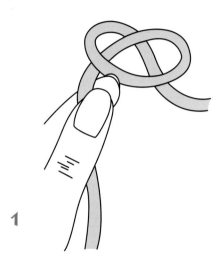

1

Insert the crochet hook and draw the loop onto the hook by pulling on the end marked A (**Fig 2**).

2

The knot should be snug on the hook but should slide easily (**Fig 3**).

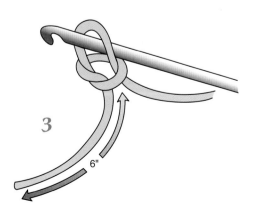

3

6"

CHAIN (CH)

The chain is the foundation on which all crochet is built. It is rather like the bottom row of a brick wall.

Hold the hook in your dominant hand and the yarn in the other hand. Take the yarn from back to front over the hook and catch it with the hook head and draw it through the slip knot on the hook (**Fig 4**).

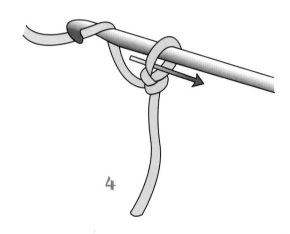

4

You have now made one chain stitch. Repeat this step for each additional chain required, moving your thumb and index finger up close to the hook after each stitch or two (**Fig 5**).

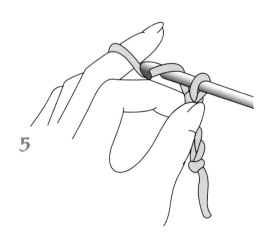

5

SINGLE CROCHET (SC)

First make a chain to the desired length.

Step 1: Insert the hook under the top loop of the 2nd chain from the hook (**Fig 6**).

Step 2: Hook the yarn, bringing the yarn over the hook from the back to the front and draw through (**Fig 7**).

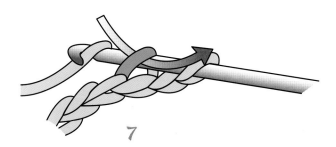

Step 3: There are now 2 loops on the hook (**Fig 8**). Take the yarn over the hook again from back to front, hook it and draw through both loops on the hook: one loop now remains on the hook and you have made one sc stitch. To make the next stitch, continue to work in this manner.

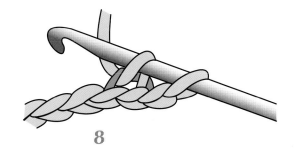

To work additional rows, chain 1 (the turning chain) and turn work counterclockwise.

Skip the turning chain and work one sc in the sc nearest your hook, inserting the hook under the top two loops of the stitch (**Fig 9**).

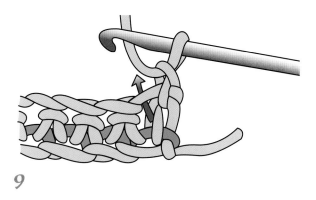

HALF DOUBLE CROCHET (HDC)

Make a chain the desired length.

Step 1: Yarn over the hook. Insert the hook into the back bump of the 3rd ch from the hook; yarn over and draw up a loop: 3 loops are now on the hook.

Step 2: Yarn over again and draw the yarn through all 3 loops on the hook at one time. You have made one hdc stitch (**Fig 10**).

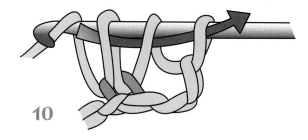

To work additional rows, make 2 chains and turn work counterclockwise. Begining in 2nd stitch (2 chains count as first half double crochet), work a half double crochet in each stitch across. Work the last stitch into the top ch; ch 1 and turn the work counter-clockwise.

DOUBLE CROCHET (DC)

Begin by making a chain the desired length.

Step 1: Bring the yarn over the hook from back to front, then insert the hook into the back bump of the fourth chain from the hook (**Fig 11**).

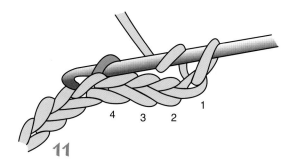

Step 2: Hook the yarn and draw it through. There are now 3 loops on the hook (**Fig 12**) .

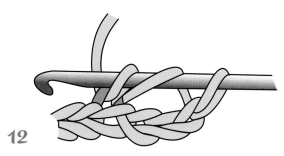

Step 3: Hook the yarn again and draw it through the first two loops on the hook. There are now 2 loops on the hook (**Fig 13**).

Step 4: Hook the yarn again and draw it through the remaining 2 loops. You have made one dc stitch. To work the next dc stitch, repeat Step 1 but insert the hook into the back bump of the next chain rather than the fourth chain from the hook. Repeat steps 2 through 4 again and continue in this manner across the row.

To work additional rows, make 3 chains and turn work counterclockwise (**Fig 14**).

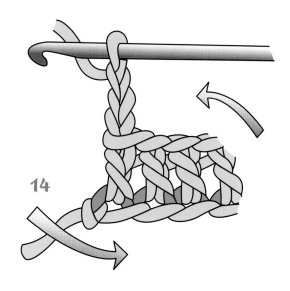

Beginning in 2nd stitch of the previous row (3 chains count as first double crochet), work a double crochet in each stitch (**Fig 15**).

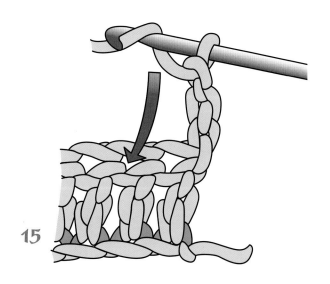

At the end of the row, work the last dc into the top chain of the turning chain of the previous row (**Fig 16**).

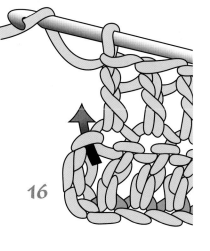

TRIPLE CROCHET (TR)

Begin by making a chain the desired length.

Step 1: Bring the yarn over the hook twice. Insert the hook into the back bump of the 5th chain from the hook (**Fig 17**).

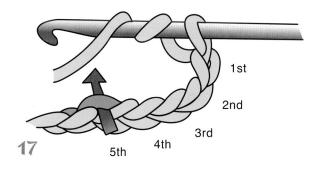

Step 2: Hook the yarn and draw through the chain. There are now 4 loops on the hook (**Fig 18**).

Step 3: Hook the yarn over again and draw through the first 2 loops on the hook. There are now 3 loops on the hook.

Step 4: Hook the yarn over again and draw through the first two loops on the hook. There are now 2 loops on the hook.

Step 5: Hook the yarn over and draw through the remaining 2 loops. You have now made one triple crochet stitch (**Fig 19**).

To work the next stitches in tr, repeat steps 1 through 5 in the back bump of each chain, working Step 1 in the next chain rather than the 4th chain from the hook.

SLIP STITCH (SL ST)

Begin by making a chain the desired length

Step 1: Insert hook in 2nd chain from the hook. Hook yarn and draw through both stitch and loop in one motion.

WORKING IN A CIRCLE

Begin by making a chain the desired length.

Step 1: Join the stitches with a sl st to form a ring (**Fig 20**).

Step 2: Chain the required stitches and work into ring or into the next stitch (**Fig 21**) .

Abbreviations & Symbols

Crochet patterns are written in a special shorthand which is used so that instructions don't take up too much space. They sometimes seem confusing, but once you learn them, you'll have no trouble following them.

These are Abbreviations

Beg	beginning
BL	back loop
BPdc	back post double crochet
BPsc	back post single crochet
Cl(s)	cluster(s)
Ch(s)	chain(s)
Cont	continue
Dc	double crochet
Dc Cl	double crochet cluster
Dc dec	double crochet decrease
Dc inc	double crochet increase
Dec	decrease
Fig	figure
FL	front loop
FPdc	front post double crochet
FPsc	front post single crochet
Hdc	half double crochet
Inc	Increase(ing)
Lp(s)	loop(s)
Patt	pattern
PC	popcorn
Prev	previous
Pst	puff stitch
Rem	remaining
Rep	repeat(ing)
Rnd(s)	round(s)
Sc	single crochet
Sc dec	single crochet decrease
Sc2tog	single crochet 3 stitches together decrease
Sl st	slip stitch
Sp(s)	space(s)
St(s)	stitch(es)
Tog	together
Tr	triple crochet
V-st	V-stitch
YO	yarn over hook

These are Standard Symbols

* An asterisk (or double asterisks**) in a pattern row, indicates a portion of instructions to be used more than once. For instance, "rep from * three times" means that after working the instructions once, you must work them again three times for a total of 4 times in all.

† A dagger (or double daggers ††) indicates that those instructions will be repeated again later in the same row or round.

: The number of stitches after a colon tells you the number of stitches you will have when you have completed the row or round.

( ) Parentheses enclose instructions which are to be worked the number of times following the parentheses. For instance, "(ch 1, sc, ch1) 3 times" means that you will chain one, work one sc, and then chain again three times for a total of six chains and three scs.

Parentheses often set off or clarify a group of stitches to be worked into the same space of stitch. For instance, "(dc, ch2, dc) in corner sp".

[ ] Brackets and ( ) parentheses are also used to give you additional information.

Terms

Front Loop—This is the loop toward you at the top of the crochet stitch.

Back Loop—This is the loop away from you at the top of the crochet stitch.

Post—This is the vertical part of the crochet stitch

Join—This means to join with a sl st unless another stitch is specified.

Finish Off—This means to end your piece by pulling the cut yarn end through the last loop remaining on the hook. This will prevent the work from unraveling.

Gauge—This simply means the number of stitches per inch, and the numbers of rows per inch that result from a specified yarn worked with a hook in a specified size. But since everyone crochets differently—some loosely, some tightly, some in between—the measurements of individual work can vary greatly, even when the crocheters use the same pattern and the same size yarn and hook.

The hook size given in crochet instructions is merely a guide and should never be used without a gauge swatch. To make a gauge swatch, crochet a swatch that is about 4" square, using the suggested hook and the number of stitches given in the pattern. Measure your swatch. If the number of stitches is fewer than those listed in the pattern, try making another swatch with a smaller hook. If the number of stitches is more than is called for in the pattern, try making another swatch with a larger hook.

The patterns in this book have been written using the crochet terminology that is used in the United States. Terms which may have different equivalents in other parts of the world are listed below.

United States	International
Double crochet(dc)	treble crochet (tr)
Gauge	tension
Half double crochet (hdc)	half treble crochet (htr)
Single crochet	double crochet
Skip	miss
Slip stitch	single crochet
Triple crochet (tr)	double treble crochet (dtr)
Yarn over (YO)	yarn forward (yfwd)
Yarn over (YO)	Yarn around needle (yrn)